Courting Mentalism (Philosophy), Religion and Literature

Courting Mentalism (Philosophy), Religion and Literature

The Core Tripartite of the Humanities

YEMI D. OGUNYEMI

RESOURCE *Publications* • Eugene, Oregon

COURTING MENTALISM (PHILOSOPHY), RELIGION, AND LITERATURE
The Core Tripartite of the Humanities

Resource Publications
An Imprint of Wipf and Stock Publishers
199 W. 8th Ave., Suite 3
Eugene, OR 97401

www.wipfandstock.com

PAPERBACK ISBN: 979-8-3852-7050-7
HARDCOVER ISBN: 979-8-3852-7051-4
EBOOK ISBN: 979-8-3852-7052-1

DEDICATED TO MY BELOVED

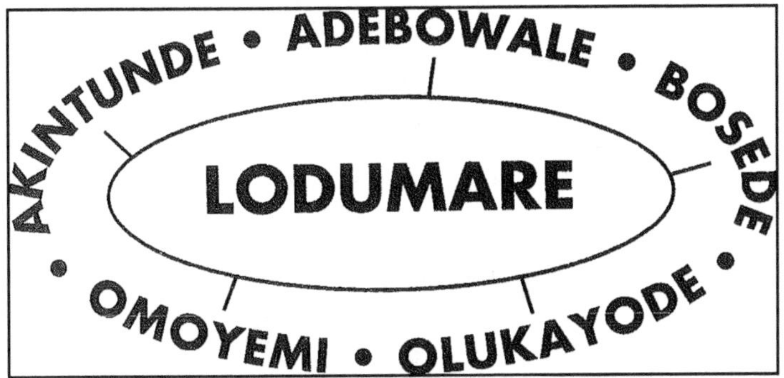

Children of the Earth
Created by Creator-Philosopher God/Olodumare
Molded by Divinity-Philosopher Obatala/Orisa-nla
Watched over by the Ancestors/Pedigrees.
fathered by the scribe.

By the same Author

Novels

The Melodrama of the Last Word
My Gazar With My Geisha
The Enchantress of Triple A
Modicums of O
Make Me Your Own
Twice Anagram
The Myths of the Coffee Boys
The Dreams of Joy
The Sweet Mother
The Talking River
The Last Cowrie Queen
The Literary Philosophy for the Year 2000
The Voice of the Earth
Ajayi Crowther's Piano

Novelettes/Novellas

The Oyo Empire
My Sworn Friends
The Demise of a Would-be Title-Holder
Pursuit of Wisdom
(Sub-Title: A Divine Story that Never Ends)

Short Stories

The Chief Who Married 35 Wives
The Yellow House
Follow Me
Aduke is a Singer, Mama
Okobaba and the Nine Angels
Tortoise, the Storyteller
Waiting for the Dry Season
Vendetta
A Divine Story that Never Ends
My Beautiful Sister
Letters from Our Empire
The Floating Bungalow
Beloved, Be Great Again
How Leke Rescued Keke
Verism, Crowns, Man and the Rule of the Fairies
Jumping Gaps of Prejudices and Racisms and the Benevolences of Robin Hood
How a Comedienne Became a Fishmonger
From the Vaudeville to the Fringe Theater
The Heroic Rescue of the Stranded Conjurer
Mourning the Loss of the Loved Ones

Poetry

Martin Luther King Jr. and Other Poems
Lagos, a City of Sisterly and Brotherly Love
Lyric-Boston, a City of Sisterly Love
The Anthologies of the Diaspora
Quid Pro Quo and Other Narratives
The African Soul
The New Talking Drum
The Dawn of Tomorrow
M-A-S-T-A-M-A-N-D-A
Sued for Paternity
Codes of Morality
The Danger of a Single Rejection
Crowns of Arts in the Calm Strength of Knowledge
The Undemocratic and Racist Amalgamation

Children's Stories

The Source of River Koku
How Dogs Become Friends of Men
Why Mother Vulture Lost Her Neck Feathers
Tortoise, the Wisest Creature
January—December Lyrics
Why Giraffes Have Long Necks
A Hut Never Hurts
Why a Cock Cannot Crow
The Belling of the Wild Cat
Why Catty-Coo Chases Mousy-Loo
Jumbo and Piggy
Butti and Moti
How Zebras Got Their Whites and Black Stripes
My First Dream
How Tortoise Survived the Famine in Ogba
The Muddy Glade
Why Daddy Was Called Ho, Ho, Ho
How Lulu Became a Swimmer
The Missing Child
How Kemi and Layo Started Schooling
The Postman and His Son
Tortoise, My Friend
Why Grasshoppers Hop
Time for Competition
The House an Elephant Built
A Day with a Hunter
My Daddy's Sweet Potatoes
How Hoody and Hoofy Became Soccer Players
How the Lion Became the King of the Beasts
Why & How the Elephant Got His Huge Ears

The Ostrich and the Boomerang
Talk to me, I am Listening, O Angel
The Bee that Keeps her Promise
Why Jako Shoots without Missing
My Neighbor's Diary
Long Live the Queen
Mama, Let Me Be Me
The Song of a River
Why Bullying is Not Good
How the Hen Made the Cock a Happy Crower
When the Children Are Difficult to Teach
Mom, It Is An Improper Overtaking
How Maria and Bobby Became Friends
The Bald Valley Village
How Honey Came To the World
Crowns of Arts in the Calm Strength of Knowledge
How Cowries Came the World
How Mother Kakapo Became a Flightless Bird
How the Horned Mother Centipede Lost Her Silver Horns

Actualities

Yoruba Idealism
Literatures of the African Diaspora
Introduction to Yoruba Philosophy, Religion and Literature
Yoruba Philosophy and the Seeds of Enlightenment
The Birth of a Child in a Fishing Boat
The Aesthetic and Moral Art of Wole Soyinka
Path to Ifetherapy and Its Healing Poems
The Literary/Political Philosophy of Wole Soyinka
Women in Europe
Media in Africa
The Political Ideas for Peace & Development in Nigeria
My Contact with Africans and Africa (Editor)
The Writers and Politics
The Birth of a Yoruba Nation
DIY-humanities
A Torrent of Abuse of Moral Philosophy and Philosophy of History

Drama

Three Plays
Obama, the Pragmatic President
(Subtitle: The Ankh of Progress)
King Oduduwa Comes to Americas and Europe
From the Vaudeville to the Fringe Theater

Acknowledgement

My calabash-full and my king-size gratitude goes to Chief Tai Bola (1898–1989), who first taught me how to break, bite and chew kola nuts, and who together with my father, taught me that it is not enough to preserve what we already have, we must find means to create what we do not have.

My experience (derived from his teachings) is the upshot of this innovative research work with a history-mythological touch, in that it starts with the oral past and ends with the written present. Variants may occur even when writing within the palace of Ooni. But one thing will remain a commonplace physically and spiritually to the Northern, Southern, Western, Eastern and Central Yoruba land; and that one thing is the holy city of Ile-Ife, the mythical and non-mythical cradle of the world, worldly.

During the course of his research (1983–1997), and like every living language, a few words have infiltrated into the Yoruba language. Some of them have been anglicized here. These words are the holy gourd, ifadom, ifalogy, ifamas(e, ifamize, ifamization, ogunate, sasarawa and Yorubalogy.

By and large, these thoughts (old and new) are posthumously dedicated to Chief Tai Bola, the historian, the diviner and philosophical priest of the Atlantic Yoruba.

DEDICATION

First Dedication

Dedicated to Prince Adebowale, Princess Bosede, Prince Akintunde, Prince Olukayode and Princess Omoyemi for their regal and nonpareil patience during the years when my research happens to become my second-nature.

Second Dedication

Dedicated to the prodigious linguist of the nineteenth century, Bishop (Dr.) Samuel Ajayi Crowther for being in the vanguard of the Enlightenment of the Modern Yoruba Idealism, and for his precocity and extraordinary ingenuity and ability to translate the English Bible into Yoruba Bible, and for providing a standard orthography that helped to re-alphabetize the Yoruba language in 1842. His lame and impotent role counted as his stricture is that he helped pooh-pooh Yoruba Ifa-Ife, the Book of Enlightenment/Knowledge before colonizers.

Third Dedication

Dedicated to the Political Philosopher Obafemi Awolowo for keeping alive the ideal spirit of Bishop (Dr.) Samuel Ajayi Crowther and for pioneering and delivering many Firsts in Africa to his credit.

Fourth Dedication

Dedicated to the Nollywood shakers and movers for not forgetting their inalienable rights and ideals to their mother tongue which may become the seventh official language of the United Nations.

Fifth Dedication

Dedicated to all the converts, who by virtue of their humble pride and honor do not forget their long line of pedigrees, their living ancient culture, courtesy of Creator-Philosopher Olodumare.

Sixth Dedication

Dedicated to pre-dynastic and dynastic terracotta artist-philosophers (circa 10,000BC-900AD) whose exquisite works have endured to open up new vistas of naturalistic civilization for the present artist-philosophers.

Seventh Dedication

Dedicated to Political Philosopher Awolowo whose moral strength and integrity pioneered/authored the following: "Those who desire to reach and keep their places at the top in any calling must be prepared to do so the hard way."

Eighth Dedication

Dedicated to Chief Olusegun Obasanjo for his moral strength and for his support for the aspirations of our youths, and for happily and smartly electing to become the first ex-President of an African country to become an agriculturalist. Although his slap on the faces of the junior royals is raising eyebrows, causing bruxism and spuming borborygmus amongst the culture vultures and cultural nobilities on the African continent and in Diaspora. Does this speak volumes for a new Yoruba country?

Ninth Dedication

Dedicated to the present and the past promoters of Yoruba mentalism/ philosophy, religion and literature. Their lofty ideals have helped them obtain inestimable jewels of knowledge in the crown of wisdom.

Tenth Dedication

Dedicated to Yoruba atata (the noble scions of the Yoruba land) for promoting the indigenous (Ifa-Ife) religion as opposed to the imported, foreign religions which are still enslaving the land: making it difficult for Yoruba land to progress like China, India, South Korea, Thailand and other countries which are strong and brave enough to stand on their on their God-given feet.

Eleventh Dedication

Dedicated to the new historians who have discovered that the phrase slave trade is a camouflaged misnomer, for a trade is a business negotiated between two or more parties, adding that the main purpose of the Europeans going to West Africa was to steal artworks and West Africans. According to the historians, what replaces slave trade in the new History Book is the Stealing, (Kidnapping), Buying and Selling of human beings which lasted for about 400 (fat) years.

Twelfth Dedication

Dedicated to the Social Media for supporting reparations and our ancestors who let us comprehend that there was no cultured slave trade but Stealing (Kidnapping), Buying and Selling of the West Africans for almost 400 (fat) years. And for supporting those who extolled the practice of justice, empathy, theological virtues—faith, hope and the charity of love (Chief Awo, MLK, etc.), raising themselves to raise the world, worldly.

Thirteenth Dedicated

Dedicated to Robin Hood, the British nonpareil hero, who stole/took from the affluent to feed the hungry, whose personal stories and affection inspired the author to write several tragicomedies, including *From the Vaudeville to the Fringe Theatre.*

Principal Dedication

The Principal Dedication to which all the above is answerable is the following: Yoruba Idealism vis-à-vis Yoruba philosophy is to honor and celebrate the ideal deeds of our long line of pedigrees/ancestors in order to stir the Kingdom of Thought and the Kingdom of Reason of the present and the future researchers, scholars and the general public.

What My Parents Told Me

DURING MY FORMATIVE YEARS, between the age of 5 and 13, when I was enjoying the benefits of juvenilia—carving, weaving and drawing, my parents (adept in classic fairytales, waxy merry as DIY artists who learn by practice and become masters by learning), told me that King Oduduwa was the first patriotic scion of the Yoruba country. They let me know that he is/was a noble man with nobiliary particles, born in the celestial Throne of Grace and re-born in the awe-inspiring settlement of Ile-Ife which is today known as the holy city of Ile-Ife, a city of over 500,000 stakhanovite inhabitants, in the present-day Yoruba land (country), flowing with organic milk and honey. King Oduduwa was a humble and gentleman, made to the character of a devout, happy in everything but putting no more faith in anything than the Book of Enlightenment—the Ifa-Ife Divination. According to them, not without some pregnant constructions, his dynasty was crème de la crème, peaceful, artistic and very resourceful throughout his reign of many decades with the benefit of the holy gourd, *the holy gourd of longevity, wellness and happiness.*

"Treat everyone with love and respect. We are the same from the same Family Tree, from the same umbilical cord of muliebrity/motherhood, from the taproot of the Family Tree to its apex. Therefore, regard everyone as your brother, sister, prince or princess. We are the same one blue blood from Oduduwa dynasty," they asserted with perfect aplomb.

My parents did not only put me wise to it, they succeeded in putting me up to it by adjuring me to break ranks with any pedantry (chop logic) and my solipsistic narrow-mindedness. They added that I should have an algorithmic knowledge of all the major divinities who are theophorically connected to Creator-Philosopher Olodumare. These theophoric divinities are Oduduwa, Obatala, O'Sango, Ogun, Orunmila, O'Yemoja, Osun, O'Sopona, Oya, O'Esu, Olokun and Ososi. They enjoined me to believe in arts, adding that art (including the chiaroscuro and the Day-Glo), a marvel of ingenuity, a symbol of reality, is an expression of happiness, an application of human creative skill. They constantly remind me that Creator-Philosopher Olodumare is an inimitable designer-artist who designed all the creatures. Knowing that there is an artist in every household in Yoruba land, and believing that art is made for life's sake and not for art's sake, I said to my parents that it suits my book to become an artist and belong to the league or class of intellectuals and artistic virtuosity. Cornucopian smiles of innocent conscience flirted with my five senses, impelling me to compare myself to a cognate object, because a cognate object is an object that is related in origin and sense to the verb governing it, as in *live a good life*.

As I grew up year by year, I understand that I, like other artists have to work within Nature's purview. Also, it becomes opalescent clear to me that of all aesthetic things/arts on the surface of the earth and under the vault of heaven, none is as aesthetic as the art-rainbow.

The Revelation of the Nonpareil Storyteller: My parents adjured me to respect the nonpareil teller whose mononymous name is Ijapa, imbued with a three-man personality—angel, fairy and human being, and to always pay homage to him. According to them, mononymous Ijapa is versed in **myth and weave**. It was the literary and artistic movement in Yoruba country in circa 9th century when every myth and weave was thought to be the divine will of Olorun/Olodumare (amuwa Olorun/Olodumare). It was the period of oral literature when mononym was the order of the day. (It was a pre-soft-pedaling revolution but Ijapa lets us know that it was a pre-artistic revolution in Yoruba country).

How Did It Start? It started when the heads of the people (full of mints of ideas filtering through people's minds) were merry with myths and artistic works, when there was an artist in every household, when the literary arts could not be taken for triviality; the society began to find happiness and the meaning of life in their mythological tales and artworks. This happiness and meaningful life led to the soft-pedaling movement which is known as myth and weave. It has since then become a tradition segueing from those oral recording and experience to the present age of pen and paper.

With stress and rhythm, cognate with the admission that learning is a cumulative process, it was a novel dawn in the life of a nation, and what's more, the 9th century symbolizes the age when aesthetics is regarded the appreciation of philosophy of nature, beauty and arts.

They emphasized that mononymous Ijapa was the greatest storyteller Yoruba country has ever produced. By the time he paid his debt to Nature (many keepers of traditions inferred that he did not die but disappeared like fairies) in the twelfth century, he was credited with thousands of tales/stories.

This is what mononymous Ijapa said of himself, "With respect to my lung power, and while taking care of number one, I am the folk hero and the fabled protagonist of antiquity of Yoruba folktales. I am no skeleton dragged out of the shadows to dance a bone dance in the middle of the leading strings. Those who know my long history will vouchsafe for me that I am a downright folk philosopher who works like a Stakhanovite since the days of pre-dynasty."

The following is his prose experience with the crown of jewels: The crown of jewels whose opalescent jewels shine in the shine of the moon, whose first gleams of the morning sun glitter upon the earth, has a metaphorical history of crowning many heads of our Oyo Emperors. It had extolled the practice of love in Yoruba country. It had served as the emblem of unity and solidified the kingdom of the holy city of Ile-Ife and reinforced the Staff of Creation. This crown of opalescent jewels, thou art the crown that gives birth to other crowns.

I was so delighted and grateful to my kind-loving parents. Because I was delighted and grateful, I was tempted to turn a verb into a verbal noun, otherwise known and called a gerund. My fund of humor came to a happy remembrance with a warm and delicious dish of taramasalata and bouillabaisse.

My Sub Rosa and Personal Dedication to Ijapa

DEDICATED TO THE NONPAREIL storyteller whose mononymous name is Ijapa: he will always be remembered as my great teacher. He put me through Yoruba fairytales and folklore, and stories with ends and stories without ends. He lets me know that every letter of the Yoruba alphabet (from A-Y), has a story attached to it, and every face has 1,000 magical stories. This makes me think mononymous Ijapa has a predilection to magic like the fairies, the small/diminutive beings with magic powers.

My intellectual and artistic virtuosity is not complete without appreciating Ijapa as the greatest fabulist that ever lived in Yoruba country. Mononymous Ijapa whose poetic name is Protatoise is the folk hero and the fabled protagonist of antiquity of the Yoruba folktales. He is noted for his legal fiction, his polite fiction, his folk etymology and his folk memory. Additionally, his epistemology of the Yoruba culture is far-reaching, making one feel that he knows many things much as he cultivates many things pertaining to the Yoruba cultural values. Although he was a grandiloquent paradox of a teller, he was nonetheless a thinking thinker who essays to avoid and deracinate many farragoes of nonsense or useless knowledge (smattering) that had marred his reputation, for so long, as an inimitable teller imbued with blue blood or a teller from the royal house. Acting like a sponger in the house of hospitality and living in genteel poverty was unregal and ridiculous, demonstrative of his bag-eyed behavior. Because of this singular behavior, his critics regard him as a cockalorum adept in cunnings and dissimulations whose prosopographies make him a queer specimen of humanity.

Author's Lodestar and Abridged Memoir

(The Calm Strength of Literary Philosophy)

If I should occupy myself by remembering the land of great antiquities, if I should recount all the artistic and the literary pleasures derived from my years of innocence, cognate with tableaux, if I should reflect upon the pleasures of memory and imagination from the years of childhood, I would feel full of vim due to my adrenaline glands. Grateful I am. I will feel sublime from inside to the outside and from outside to the inside, as though the descendants of the slavers had settled the reparations for purloining our ancestors from the continent of blue blood. My appetite for literature (my propaedeutic genre) will continue to increase, as I grow from year to year, while my appetite for comestible will be controlled or circumscribed by the pleasures obtained from the reams of writings. For good literature, which is the foundation of pleasures (like music rather than the media) nourishes the human emotions, reaffirms the present and reconstructs the future. These ethical and rational beliefs and assertions are inexhaustibly fundamental and interesting by the contents of their canons of conduct.

Relating all this with mankind and seeking the pleasures of relationships are the greatest sources of happiness that one can derive from the calm strength of humanity, regaling upon the virtue of philosophy, literature and arts, yes—true to the province of aesthetics.

The calm strength of love, found in humanity and the feeling of writing, dovetailing with the artistic virtuosity is like the feeling derived from listening to the delicious music of the spheres. An intellectual had asked, "Why do you write?" I write because my writing could become one of the soft-pedaling means to promote/enhance peace and love around the world. I write because the mortals and immortals expect me to write. I write because I want to be read, and read others. I write because I have fallen head over heels in love with letters, books and the power of words. I write because Creator-Philosopher Olodumare is my teacher and my director and my giver who always gives me mints of ideas that filter through my mind. I write because I invariably find an organic happiness in writing. I write because writing qualifies me to belong to the class/league of sciences and the humanities. I write because writing therapeutically distils my mind. I write because I want my writing to belong to the archives and libraries of immortality. I write because writing helps me link my existence to saints, angels, geniuses and heroes. I write because I want the Oversoul to explain to me why there are so many mysteries and tragicomedies in the world. I write because I want my writing to refresh the memories of the loved ones whose departures make my heart trapped in melancholy. I write in order to know myself and what myself can do to help everyone, my neighbor, since everyone is my friend with the charity of love. I write because I want my writing to inform, enlighten, entertain, educate, inspire, charm/enchant, and above all, inoculate the world with the ingredients of wellness, corporeal and spiritual happiness, likened to the thrills of a sweet dream.

On noticing that I am still one-third a writer I would love to be, my parents who always stand on ceremony, in their hours of happiness, nobility, pleasantries and gleam of humor, demand of me the loftiest, the best, the crème de la crème, the noblest and the most supreme that I can do, but much that I could by no possibility have done, in order to belong to the league/class of sciences and the humanities, and be guided by the literary philosophy, and the power of words, as reason guides the human soul to nirvana or sasarawa.

Yemi D. Ogunyemi, Prof. (also known as Yemi D. Prince)
(Literary Philosopher)

Foreword

Courting Mentalism (Philosophy), Religion and Literature

FROM OUR GROUND-BREAKING RESEARCH, we are able to find the vistas of bygone times. These vistas of bygone times speak to the discovery that opens up new vistas. Some researchers may call the vista an age of eclaircissement or enlightenment but we will call it Ifa-Ife Divination, Book of Enlightenment or the Book of Knowledge. We acknowledge the fact that it is a new world, discovered in the 21st century. This ground-breaking research lets us know what is called "Slave Literature." This is clear to every literary historian without the use of meta-language or double entendre, and without any concern of gimmick or gibberish. Although this is not the focus of *Courting Mentalism, Religion and Literature*, however it is good to mention it as an addendum to the Foreword.

The Yoruba people already have experienced the colonial literature and post-colonial literature, dovetailing with their autochthonous religion and philosophy but they do not experience anything about the slave literature that spread over a period of 400 years, from circa 1500 to 1900. This was the period when nothing was covered either by the Yoruba people or by the slavers and their kings. It was a period of complete oral literature. And we cannot blame anyone but appreciate humanity that evolves every generation.

The so-called commercial slave trade, otherwise known as the trade of stealing, buying and selling human beings occurred when the Yoruba people existed without the calm strength of reading and writing as we know it today. As we know it today, the slave literature is called oral literature and its oral people with the oral knowledge of events. These uprooted Yoruba people still don't forget the inhumanity and the intemperate languages of the slavers such as "Except for their artworks, we do not need their names, nor do we need their intelligence, understanding, wisdom and knowledge. All we need from them is the strength of their arms and their weariless shanks."

Lo and behold! Whenever the literary historians blamed the West Africans for not doing enough to defend their own, the West Africans would retort by saying that the slavers were often intimidating with their guns in hands: adding that they talked and walked upon their land as if they were the owners of their land and the universe.

This will startle one and all. As the winds of change are blowing, as we cannot resist the spirit of the times/zeitgeist, let us ask a quick question: Where today can we find these uprooted people with their mentalism, religion and literature? They can be found in countries such as Argentina, Antigua-Barbuda, Bahamas, Barbados, Belize, Bermuda, Bolivia, Brazil, Canada, Cayman Islands, Colombia, Costa Rica, Cuba, Dominica, Dominican Republic, El Salvador, French Guyana, French Polynesia, Grenada, Guadeloupe, Guatemala, Guyana, Haiti, Honduras, Jamaica, Mexico, Panama, Paraguay, Peru, Puerto Rico, Saint Kitts and Nevis, Saint Lucia, Suriname, United States, Venezuela, Virgin Islands. The people of these countries who have some philosophical, religious and literary ties to Yoruba country had depended on their verbal memories for so many years, until now. Now we have some Yoruba centers in Brazil, Cuba, Trinidad and Tobago, the United States and a good few. Of all these Yoruba centers, Oyotunji African Kingdom in Shelton, South Carolina is perhaps the most prominent, the most dynamic and the most best-selling. It is one of the most unique kingdoms in the world, just as unique as the Holy See or the Vatican City in the City of Rome, Italy. These bodacious references are based upon Slave Literature. Whether it is Slave Literature or Slave History, its Day-Glo and the chiaroscuro are the same and the Yoruba people cannot envision enough of it. They are based upon slavery—the stealing, buying and selling of the human beings by the Europeans. Any attempt to ignore slave literature or to pooh-pooh it, is not our notion of moral civilization, cognate with the calm strength of humanity. Certainly, it is not our notion to pretend that the trade in stealing, buying and selling humanity was not as tempestuous as it was hemorrhagic.

The Yoruba written culture may refer to the zeitgeist, to the things of the present. But we must recognize that Yoruba culture (the cultivated culture), embracing primarily philosophy, religion and literature is known to be very encyclopedic in nature. That the viva voce or oral culture is antecedent to the written culture cannot be discountenanced. This means the utility and the folkways of the past cannot be ignored as meaningless. Without placing the present over the past, it is our research, a ground-breaking one, on oral culture that led to the myths and weave, the literary and artistic movement in the 9th century monarchical Yoruba country. Unarguably, that movement is one of the earliest of its kind in the world, worldly. Its publication as an eBook in 2024 justifies its importance as a research work that spans both the academic and the trade market.

Another research work of interest whose publication will demonstrate how important the slave literature is, is The Stealing, Buying and Selling of My Great, Great Grandparents, a book that speaks to the author's kith and kin who were stolen in the 1750s.

Introduction

> Diffusion of knowledge is made possible through books and mythologies on many areas of learning, notably philosophy, history, literature and religion.
>
> REUBEN O. OGUNYEMI (1900–1970)

A CUTTING-EDGE RESEARCH AND RESEARCH METHODOLOGY

It is always my thrill of joy and my hope that I will find an answer in whatever I set out to do. This is why I set out at dawn just before the first cock-a-doodle-doo. Why did I set out so early without my breakfast? It is because of my cutting-edge research on *Courting Mentalism, Religion and Literate* which is new and stands the chance of being adopted into an academic course or discipline. Juxtaposing three areas of learning may not be meaningful if its chiaroscuro is not inexhaustibly delightful, meritorious and interesting.

A RESEARCHER

A researcher is someone who uses research methodology to gather data. Will my cutting-edge research lead me to success? It will lead me to success because a research is a systematic investigation into and study of materials and sources in order to establish facts and reach new conclusions. In a similar vein, a research is a creative and systematic work undertaken to increase the stock of knowledge. It involves the collection, organization and the analysis of evidence to increase the understanding of a topic, characterized by a particular attentiveness to controlling sources of bias and error.

RESEARCH METHODOLOGY

Is a research methodology relevant in your investigation? Yes. A research methodology is relevant and indeed crucial in my investigation. For a research methodology is the specific procedure or technique used to select, identify, process and analyze information about a topic in a research paper/document, allowing the reader to critically evaluate a study's overall validity and reliability.

Since there are two types of researches—nonfiction academic research and creative fiction research, it is incumbent on me to long for nonfiction academic research which is sometimes called a fast-pedaling research, while creative fiction research is sometimes called a soft-pedaling research. One thing is certain. It is certain that my research will remain unique, innovative, assuming all the qualities needed to call it a cutting-edge research. There is no gainsaying the obvious that the publication of *Courting Mentalism, Religion and Literature* will be a welcome and useful summation to the academia, cognate with Yoruba and non-Yoruba who are interested in the encyclopedic nature of Yoruba culture.

Courting Yoruba Mentalism (Philosophy) Religion and Literature is an upshot of the four innovative research projects carried out at HU—Harvard University, BU—Boston University, NU—Northeastern University, UMASS—University of Massachusetts, Boston, between 1994 and 2010. The first research project is *Literatures of the African Diaspora*, published in 2004. The second research project is *The Literary/Political Philosophy of Wole Soyinka*, published in 2009. The third research project is *The Oral Traditions in Ile-Ife*, published in 2010. The fourth research project, to be published is *Courting Mentalism (Philosophy), Religion and Literature,* my full cup of contentment, and the full cup of contentment for the researchers, especially the new researchers who are beginning to find both the national and international research projects whole, meaningful, and inexhaustibly interesting.

Two areas of human interests which have made this project complete, meaningful, and inexhaustibly interesting are mentalism and humanism, impelled, compelled and propelled by creative thinking, and DIY-humanities which is a passion for innovation, discovery and a desire to learn independently. Creative Thinking in its facile definition is the combination of research ideas and literary experiences, and transforming those research ideas into new ways of reasoning, thinking and writing. Sharing a common thread but different definitions, mentalism in its self-definition is the theory that the physical and the psychological phenomena are ultimately only explicable in terms of a creative and interpretative mind. But humanism, the gamut of the milk of human kindness, describes itself as a philosophical and moral outlook or stance that emphasizes the value and divine love of (milk of human kindness) human beings, individually and collectively.

As literature segues into culture, so does culture into literature. Both can whisper without the other. The segueing or the flowing of literature into culture and vice versa is melodramatic. While culture is the totality of man, literature is the art that portrays that totality. Therefore, one can mirror man through his culture as one can view him through his literature. It is the literature that connects the toes to the hold, the Mother Nature. Literature lights the way as mentalism/philosophy throws a reflective ray upon that way. While Divinity-Philosopher Obatala molds man out of clay, Divinity-Philosopher Ogun clears the way for that clay-made man for his toes to have a firm grip upon the earth with a natural certainty.

If Creator-Philosopher Olodumare is our witness and the witness of all the demythologized divinities, one is convinced that the encyclopedic nature of Yoruba culture is shrouded in myths and mythologies, embracing directly or indirectly mentalism/philosophy, psychology, history, anthropology, mathematics, cosmology, cosmogony, herbalogy and autochthonous divinatory religion. Nigerian culture is a culture in diversity. It is like a table which until now has been standing on three legs—Yoruba, Hausa and lgbo. Other legs have been acquired and added to it because other ethnic groups also want to portray their religions, philosophies and literary values.

When the Nigerian government succeeded in partitioning the country into 36 political states, they did not forget the diversity of the ethnic groups. What they forgot are the literary imprints of the main linguistic divisions in the country. Is it not ethnically and diachronically discernible that the mentalism, the autochthonous religion and the literary traditions of the Yoruba people are not the same as either the Igbo's or the Fulani/Hausa's? Is it not true to say that Nigeria has more than one mentalism, one religion, one literary tradition? To pretend to have the knowledge of this fact is to succumb to the temptation that there is no value in the creating of the states. To pretend that Nigeria has only one mentalism, one religion and one literary tradition is to ignore the fact that the only thing that synchronically binds Nigeria together is her lingua franca, English language, which is now becoming the mother tongue for any person who has been speaking and writing it for at least half a century.

If Creator-Philosopher Olodumare is my protector, you will see with one eye what I have seen with half an eye. Talking of this vast land of rainy and dry seasons: what does the land have in common but necklaces of beads? Two or three nations, at least, between whom there is no intercourse and no murmur of seriousness, who are ignorant of each other's habits and cardinal virtues—love, morality, temperance, honor, honesty, prudence, justice, braveryand fortitude, a nation that exists as though the citizens are dwellers in different time zones, or inhabitants of different planets, who are formed in disunity by a different homo sapiens, who are fed by a different repast, who are characterized by different manners and etiquettes, and not governed by the same laws and mentalism, and not by the same bents for statuary arts. This is the beautiful country of mean infrastructural developments where some of the intellectually-equipped minds are circumscribed, and some bullied as indolent.

Raising hue and cry against the slow Growth of Mentalism: Not many scions of the land yearn for mentalism, for autochthonous religion has not only stifled mentalism but it has also swallowed it, leaving something like gossamer as its regurgitation.

If it pleases Creator-Philosopher Olodumare, I will sue myself to take this opportunity to whisper into your mortal ears, applying the following plea: May Creator-Philosopher Olodumare guide our footsteps as reason guides the human soul. With its unknown teeming population, no leader in the first quarter of this twenty-first century can deliver one fourth of the needed infrastructure. Why are the leaders fibbing when they know they have no abilities and capabilities to deliver to the teeming masses? For example, the United Kingdom had a population of approximately 27 million during the Industrial Revolution in the 1850s. And she delivered to the gusto of the populace. Today, there is no leader who can deliver even if that leader is intellectually-equipped. The sole and soulful solution for our snail-like progress is devolution of power to the regions/states and let the regional leader prove or show his mettle, or else be removed by the hue and cry. Nigeria is overdue for an infrastructural revolution!

Why should Yoruba have their cultural toes and lips in other parts of the world? Is because of the domino theory? Why were they prone to slavery and colonization in spite of their almighty wealth of experience and bullet-proof armies? Is it because divination is trans-cultural? The monosyllabic yes or no of the answer is out of the question. According to the matriarchs and patriarchs of the land, the Chiefs and keepers of traditions were enjoying abundance, and out of plenitude, they were tempted to join their West African counterparts, practicing domestic slavery. Divinity-Philosopher Orisanla, on seeing that the practice was immoral and ungodly, called on Ifa-Ife philosopher, divinity-philosopher Orunmila. Divinity-philosopher Orunmila, the cultivator of Ifa-Ife Divinization then passed the message on to the ewi poet, saying they should put the kibosh on the domestic slavery but they did not hearken to the voice of their Creator. Divinity-Philosopher Orisanla was ireful and said, "My creatures have disobeyed their Creator. Shall I spank them with the Staff of Creation? Or shall I spank them with *ase*?"The comeuppance of their disobedience was the scattering of their sons and daughters across the seas and oceans during the Middle Passage. The aesthetics and the flowering genius of the kingdoms were no more. The time of plenty was no more. The spirit of the land seemed to have been enervated.

What the outside world means to Yoruba land is what the Yoruba land means to the outside world. When the Yoruba man speaks of the rising sun in *ilaorun*(east), he does not reconcile the expression with Copernican system of astronomy. What he means is as true under Copernican system as it is true under Ptolemaic system. When he says the Yoruba land is the mirror of the ancient world, he is not swallowing his words just because other cultures can utter such a poetic expression. Yoruba Ifa will continue to search for its past even if we know of the institutional classification of the fourteenth and fifteenth centuries artists in the sacred city or the holy city of Ile-Ife. Man's intellect is given to him to investigate the nature of both the physical and the spiritual world around him.

What could have happened if the gods and goddesses in the philosophy of Hinduism had been brought to the brink of extinction? What could have happened if Ifa which embraces polytheism and dualism had been replaced by Christianity? What could have happened if the Greek deities and mythologists had been banished or diasporized by an unorthodox apostate, yearning for a new civilization of worship? Again, the pros and cons are out of the question. No one could tell precisely what could have happened. One thing is certain. It is certain that when an Orisa or ancestor/pedigree rebukes his or her followers, the followers will find it difficult to enjoy their palmy days.

It is those palmy days of the Yoruba people the papers inside this cover intend to elucidate, hermeneutically. By so doing, the papers will dally with the affections of mentalism (philosophy), the religion and the literary traditions of the Yoruba land, from oral status to literacy. (In agreement with the title of this book, the papers will be courting mentalism (philosophy), religion (including the religious/theological virtues—faith, hope and charity of love) and the literary traditions of the Yoruba people, with a few double entendres, from the oral status to the written status).

Mentalistically—Philosophically, the search for the knowledge in respect of the Yoruba people, depends on the calm strength of their cultural or folk philosophy. For Yoruba mentalism/philosophy is a narrative, cultural or folk philosophy explicating and pointing to the knowledge of the causes and the nature of things affecting the corporeal and the spiritual universe and its wellness. As the diffusion of knowledge through books and lectures regarding Yoruba mentalism is becoming prevalent, the need to strike the keynote before we proceed to pursue the tune, is imperative, for our samskara and ability to pursue the tune is our samskara and ability to winnow the truth from falsehood, knowing that a folk philosophy is the philosophy of a people, depicting their nine cardinal virtues, namely, love, morality, temperance, honor, honesty, bravery, prudence, justice and fortitude. The Yoruba society is heaven and heaven cannot be too far from *sasarawa* (paradise). The Yoruba man believes that if his days on the surface of the earth are blessed, his hereafter will equally be blessed. Creator-Philosopher God is the center of existence, of everything one has; of everything attainable and unattainable. He is the beginning and the end of the earth. Yoruba philosophy also teaches one that man is here for a reason. It encourages one not to judge the appearance but the inside. The mentalism/philosophy, in its delta formation, empties itself into an ocean of religion whose subdivisions are cosmogony and cosmology. Because philosophy gives birth to religion, it is believed that the earliest Ife dwellers philosophized for 256 days before they inferred that Ife and its people would not die a premature death. Some moral philosophers verbalize that is probably why Ifa-Ife Divination has 256 OduIfa Mentalistic cum Literary Corpus, and each OduIfa stands for 800 stories, rich in aphorisms, syllogisms and apologues. If 256 OduIfa should be multiplied by 800, the mathematical result will be 204, 800 stories, making use of ori—head which is the definition of the body, the substrate unto which other parts of the body are answerable. Inductively, mentalism and religion seem to emanate from the same kingdom of thought and kingdom of reasoning.

Metaphysically, all our propaedeutic research work lets us know that mentalism/philosophy is an enhancer, a promoter of eclaircissement/enlightenment and rationality. Mentalism adds fullness to the meaning of life. That being said, let's start by saying that we must remember that a lateral thinker is a thinking thinker. Conversely, a thinking thinker is a lateral thinker. With the logic of a philosopher (a thinking thinker), one is equipped to know how to pinch out the lateral buds to get large chrysanthemum blooms.

The dilemma faced by many mentalists/philosophers is that there are many rhetorical questions which may be asked, and when asked, they are likened to philosophical questions, which like the rhetorical questions, are searching for answers. Mentalists/Philosophers and lay philosophers are still searching for answers for the following questions that recur every day throughout the world:

(1) Why are we here on earth?

(2) Why should we die?

(3) Why is it that Air, one of the four elements is invisible?

(4) Did the world evolve or was it created?

(5) How are creatures (including human beings), artistically designed?

Certainly, you are a mentalist/philosopher, a thinking thinker if any of those five questions has ever filtered through your mind. With a bodacious conviction, cognate with a philosophical diction, nothing will stop you from saying that you are a mentalist/philosopher. For, according to Yoruba philosophy, any lore that widens people's horizons and presents food for thought is the beginning of philosophy.

May what is true be true

May what is perceived to be dangerous not be dangerous

May what is paradoxical be paradoxical

May the absolute one not be a ruthless one

May what is moral or ethical be moral or ethical

May philosophers be enhancers and promoters of eclaircissement/enlightenment and rationality.

Standing as an accretion to the above and serving as a metaphysical discovery that opens up new vistas is that the earth breathes endlessly. Her breathing under the feet of every human being is a "breath of life" which is why every human being is reluctant to desecrate the earth. With a perceptible nod of approval, one can verbalize that every down-to-earth society like the Yoruba land believes in exobiology. When two Elders sit and start playing ayo game, they are said to be relishing their axiomatic bliss. When an Elder is seen playing with a youth, he is said to be enjoying his green old age. Essentially, out of 256 books of oral philosophies, more than half of them are derived from axioms. In other words, they are philosophical axioms or aphorisms. In Yoruba land, philosophy is everything you touch, and everything you touch can be versed into mentalism or philosophy. We have no means to measure the distant past but Chief Obafemi Awolowo's disciplined political-philosophical dogmas still line the vistas of milk of human kindness: a compound or a hyphenated accretion to humanism.

Ancient Greek heritage in mentalism or philosophy is not supposed to be subjective to ignore the ancient Yoruba mentalism or philosophy, for each one of them is thoughtful, derived from the kingdom of reason and the kingdom of thought. As far as the author could remember, whenever his father, Reuben O. Ogunyemi (circa 1900–1970), spoke in a language that derailed the calm strength of his understanding, his father would say Yoruba language philosophy can be too inexhaustible to comprehend.

However, he believed that Yoruba alphabet is an immortal alphabet. It is not to be disrupted or altered. Any attempt to alter it will certainly lead to a hay of confusion to the Yoruba language, for the alphabet is a set of letters or symbols in a fixed order, used to represent the basic sounds of a language, in particular the set of letters from A to Y in the case of the Yoruba alphabet, and from A to Z in the case of the English alphabet.

By virtue of induction, and by considering their humble and calm strength of knowledge, both divinity-philosophers Oduduwa and Orunmila subscribe to the fact that mathematics is everything in life inasmuch as there are additions, divisions, multiplications and subtractions in every day of our life. Numerically, they would expound that 30 is a common multiple of 2, 3, 5, 6, 10 and 15, while 28 is a multiple of 7.

On getting to the top of one's bent in life, one should not forget to illuminate or enlighten the world about all the branches of mentalism, and if need be, whisper into the immortal ears of the standby fairies and let them perceive and comprehend that a man can be as great a fairy-like magician as he likes as long as he does not set the world ablaze or set a bad example of enchanting the entire world into a fairyland where the whole world will be impelled or compelled to alchemize base metals into gold, silver and bronze. Let such a man seek the lofty ideals and find the inestimable jewels of knowledge in the crown of wisdom.

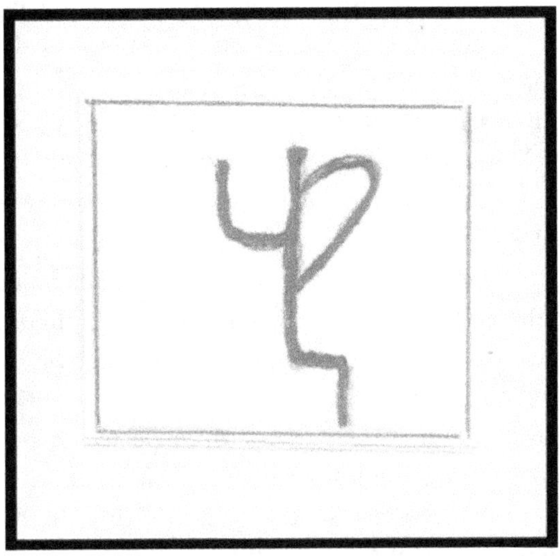

Symbol of Yoruba Philosophy

IMPORTANCE OF MENTALISM

In order to comprehend how important mentalism is, it is pertinent and indeed proper to understand what mentalism is. Mentalism has a broad definition and a compact definition. In its broad definition, mentalism/philosophy covers everything we do that is preceded by rational thinking. In this wise, mentalism/philosophy is an act of reasoning. Like mathematics which is everything in life, mentalism/philosophy is indispensable. So, it is convincingly evident to verbalize that it is everything that broods over rational reasoning, for if we should allow our argument to be the line of our reason, and the line of our reason the pith of our argument, we will perceive that mentalism/philosophy has many branches such as ethics, mentalism, idealism, morality, aestheticism, and so on.

The compact definition of mentalism/philosophy goes thusly. Mentalism is the rational investigation of the truths and principles of beings, knowledge or conduct. It has three classical branches, namely natural philosophy, moral philosophy and metaphysical philosophy upon which mentalism/philosophy is built or carved, upon a marble stone, if so desired.

In addition to the compact definition, mentalism/philosophy is the use of reason and argument in seeking truth and knowledge of reality, especially of the causes and nature of things, and of the principles governing existence, the material universe, perception of the physical phenomena and human behavior.

The question many of us like to ask is: what is the use or importance of philosophy? Many institutions encourage the teaching and studying of mentalism/philosophy because mentalism or philosophy enhances the mind and widens one's horizons. Additionally, philosophy increases one's happiness, especially if one is passionately fond of mathematics and able to realize that mathematic, an integral part of mentalism/philosophy is indispensable, inasmuch as one makes use of addition, subtraction, multiplication and division on a daily basis.

Moreover, mentalists/philosophers are expected to be the hatchers and bearers of reasoning and knowledge, capable of sanitizing the world, liberating the mind and emboldening or motivating the human race to achieve its potential—scientifically, technologically, spiritually and corporeally. A math-philosopher will quickly let us know that 30 is a common multiple of 2, 3, 5, 6, 10, and 15, while 28 is a multiple of 7.

Philosophy has many areas or components that consist of the use of reason and argument in seeking truth and knowledge, one of them is mentalism. Mentalism is the theory that the physical and the psychological phenomena are ultimately only explicable in terms of a creative and interpretive mind.

Talking of a creative and interpretive mind, I will regard myself a learner who believes that learning is a cumulative process. Granted that the spirit of the foregoing is comprehensively followed, granted that I understand and subscribe to algorithmic thinking (nay algorithmic logic), I have every reason to be compared to a cognate object, because a cognate object is an object that is related in origin and sense to the verb governing it , as in *live a good life.*

YORUBA PHILOSOPHY AND YORUBALOGY BASED UPON LITERARY PHILOSOPHY

Tojutoju (my nephew) whose reams of writings are based on Yoruba folk, cultural or literary philosophy is the seventh writer to stand upon the podium on the seventh day of the melodramatics as related to mentalism. He argued that the literary philosophy of the littoral people of the Yoruba land is a tripartite of literature, philosophy and the autochthonous religion of Oduduwa land. All the areas of the Atlantic Yoruba are heuristically progressive in purpose and in passion, constituting the society in which the people are drawn into contiguity like the siblings. He had written widely on Yoruba philosophy across the board, and during the last five years, he had been giving lectures on this very subject which has inspired many citizens of the Atlantic Yoruba. Today, his paper is entitled "Yoruba Philosophy and Yorubalogy." *Yoruba Philosophy and Yorubalogy* is also the title of his forthcoming book on the subject.

"I will be brief as a lip of a saucer inasmuch as my samskara permits me to do so. So let me start by saying that the geography of this nation is like two nations," said Tojutoju, "between which there is no unconditional love and philosophical goal." The citizens are ignorant of each other's habits, thoughts, emotions and psychologies, as though they are dwellers in different zones, or inhabitants of different planets, who are formed from different Homo sapiens, fed by a different repast and ordered by different manners and are not governed by the same laws. This is the land from which a new Yoruba land (a beau monde) hopes, prays to emerge with all the ingredients that can translate into a meaningful life.

"The supernova vista of enlightenment/eclaircissement has given birth to an innovative research whose title is Yorubalogy", said Tojutoju. Yorubalogy which is the brainchild of myths and weave, is described as the general and academic study of subjects such as anthropology, ethnology, history, language, literature, philosophy, psychology, sociology, mathematics, works of art and other areas of human interests of the Yoruba people on the African continent and in Diaspora. In the near future, it may embrace other "ological studies." (Myths and weave is the literary and artistic movement in the 9th century monarchical Yoruba country).

Under the umbrella of Creative Thinking (which essentially is the combination of research ideas and the literary experiences and transforming them into new ways of thinking, reasoning and writing) Yorubalogy is intended to be included in the curriculums of colleges and universities in Yoruba land. Its inclusion will enable us to learn more about African, African-American Studies, African, African-Australasian Studies, African, European-Studies, African, Latin-American Studies and African, West-Indian Studies. This novel curriculum, entitled Yorubalogy will enhance our knowledge of history and ideology of our African kith and kin spread all over the six continents of the world, worldly. It is fundamental to understand their historical and literary tie to Africa, now and in the distant past. This is the primary vision and mission of *Literatures of the African Diaspora*, published in 2004, whose research has taken this author to the six continents of the world in search of the people of African descent.

YORUBA PHILOSOPHY/MENTALISM

What has given birth to Yorubalogy is Yoruba folk or literary Philosophy. But there are always many aspects of studies in Yorubalogy. Their aspectual conclusion is not far-fetched. For, there is little or no aspectual difference in saying "I saw Ade crossing the street" and "I saw Ade cross the street." The study Yoruba philosophy is akin to the study of Yorubalogy. Likewise, the study of Yorubalogy is akin to the study of Yoruba philosophy. This reminds me of the saying that the proper study of mankind is man. And what is Yoruba folk or literary philosophy? Yoruba folk philosophy is a narrative, cultural or folk philosophy, explicating and pointing to the knowledge of the causes and nature of things affecting the corporeal and the spiritual universe and its wellness. Generally, normatively, and considering the Yoruba prescriptive language, a folk philosophy is the cultural mentalism/ philosophy of a people, depicting their cardinal virtues—morality, love, honor, honesty, temperance, bravery, justice, prudence and fortitude. These nine cardinal virtues are the capstones or the kernels of Yoruba codes of morality in Yoruba land and in Diaspora. They speak to all the departments of the Yoruba culture in Africa and in Diaspora. They guide the footsteps of the scions of the land as reason guides the human souls or faculty—ori. They speak to every step the Yoruba people take. And they could be found in the way they eat, drink, in the way they walk, stand, sit, sleep, look, play, work, sell, buy, read, write, love, marry, cook, and in the way they greet. The codes of morality are therefore regarded the sine qua non in Yoruba land. They are the cotyledons of civility. They are the cotyledons of *iwalewa*, credited unarguably to divinity-philosopher Oshun, divinity-philosopher Orunmila, and philosopher-king Oduduwa, the progenitor of the Yoruba people, the bringer of light and the pioneer of Yoruba philosophy. In sum, the codes of morality in Yoruba philosophy are so high and precious that no one wants to go under the attack of the gourd-eyed or the bag-eyed behavior. We must stop at what *Iwalewa* stands for, otherwise we may be accused of overlabor and brachylogy.

What Philosopher Ijapa said of Divinity-Philosopher Ogun

> "There has never been an artist-philosopher greater than Ogun. There is invariably permanent happiness in every aesthetic work. Artist-philosopher Ogun taught me one important thing, this important thing, not only without turning away from, but with a greatly increased interest and ruling passion in the common feelings and common destiny of humanity."

What Philosopher Ijapa said of himself

> "I am no skeleton of a tortoise dragged out of the shadow to dance a bone dance in the middle of the leading strings. Those who know my long history of comic, dramatic and narrative performances can testify that I am a downright folk philosopher since the days of the pre-dynasty. So regard seriously the Book of Enlightenment. Those who know me can vouchsafe that I have faith in Yoruba naturalistic civilization as shown by the artworks of the artist-philosophers and their indigenous knowledge which is unique to them from generation to generation."

THE BOOK OF ENLIGHTENMENT OR THE BOOK OF KNOWLEDGE

I can say this of the Book of Enlightenment, the Ifa-Ife: if the Book of Enlightenment has not guided and saved our ancestors/pedigrees in the past, it is false; if it has guided and saved our ancestors/pedigrees in the past, it is true. What is the Book of Enlightenment or the Book of Knowledge? We may not be too quick to ask, for it is necessary to ask. In brevity, the Book of Enlightenment or the Book of Knowledge whose masthead is Ifa-Ife Divination is the philosophy cum religious book of the Yoruba people from the ancient the viva voce time to the present. Its components are philosophy, religion and literature. Other components are psychology, sociology, anthropology, ethnology, cosmogony, cosmology, mathematics, et cetera, et cetera.

Since time immemorial, mononymous Ijapa has always been an indispensable mentalist and folklorist. Mononymous Ijapa was a great thinker. As a matter of fact, he was regarded as a thinking-thinker, although he was sometimes accused of being a grandiloquent speaker. He was the folk hero and the fabled protagonist of antiquity of Yoruba folklore. He has the following to verbalize: "If one has to think like a philosopher in order to live like a philosopher, one must be ready to hug/embrace the sense of reality, for in order to find the sense of reality, one has to combine one's mentalism/philosophy of infallibility with the power to learn from one's past mistakes/ solecisms, for I realize that learning is a cumulative process."

TWO SCHOOLS OF THOUGHTS

In deference to the Schools of Thoughts fathered by Reuben O. Ogunyemi (1900–1970) and Bertrand Russell (1872–1970), respectively, we may need to explicate more on the importance of mentalism/philosophy. In his opinion, Reuben O. Ogunyemi has said that any lore that widens people's horizons and presents food for thought is the beginning of mentalism/philosophy. On the other hand, Bertrand Russell has said that to understand an age, or a nation, we must understand its philosophy, and to understand its philosophy, we must ourselves be in some degree/way philosophers/ mentalists. Both of them are right in every respect.

Our thinking, cognate with the fund of common sense, derived from our ancestors has given us two letters, M and M. Let us not demerit the first letter M because it leads us to mentalism and mentalism widens one's horizons. Equally, it enhances one's status/station in life. While the first M stands for Mentalism, the second M stands for mythology.

If for some reason we should liken mythology to an anabranch and that anabranch segues/flows into what we did not know in the distant past and what we know today, it stands to reason that mythology is antecedent to many fields of study/learning.

In Yoruba mythology, which precedes Yoruba Idealism 2022, the Yoruba people do not believe that chance controls the universe, as postulated by Charles Sanders Pierce (1839–1914), the inventor of tychism, a branch of philosophy whose theory maintains that chance controls the universe. Charles Sanders Pierce is also regarded as the father of pragmatism. From another point of view, there are many things and many instances that occur or happen by chance. A case in point is that of Dr. Samuel Ajayi Crowther (1807–1891). During some of his evangelism, he let us know that he was enslaved by chance, manumitted by chance and rose from grass to grace by chance. But in all his intellectual and scholarly speeches he never verbalized that chance controlled the universe.

In sum and substance, Charles Sanders Pierce's expounding does not represent the majority of Yoruba opinions who strongly believe that the Oversoul is the Creator of all things seen and unseen. (All things are *amuwa* Olodumare, meaning all things happen through the will of Creator-Philosopher Olodumare).

ARGUMENT, THE FUND OF COMMON SENSE

There may be no particular virtue in doing things the way they have always been done; however, there is one particular virtue in perceiving Yoruba mentalism. Let us point to a few virtues that are relevant to arguments. With stress and rhythm, let's take a look at a few arguments, cognate with mentalism and ponder over their comparative merits. Argument is a series of premises and at least one conclusion. The premises provide support for the conclusion. The following are some simple, hypothetical arguments and their fund of common sense:

(a) Head is the definition of the body (Premise 1)
All human beings have heads (Premise 2)
Therefore head is the definition of the body (Premise 3)
(Conclusion from premises 1 and 2).

(b) All Ayo game players are lateral thinkers (Premise 1)
You are versed in playing Ayo game (Premise 2)
Therefore you are a lateral thinker (Premise 3)
(Conclusion from premises 1 and 2).

(c) All the villagers can dance to talking drum music (Premise 1)
You are a villager (Premise 2)
Therefore you can dance to talking drum music (Premise 3)
(Conclusion from premises 1 and 2).

(d) All the diviners act like prophets (Premise 1)
You are a diviner (Premise 2)
Therefore you act like a prophet (Premise 3)
(Conclusion from premises 1 and 2).

Religiously, Yoruba religion is latitudinarian by nature. They ascribe to the kingdom of heaven or the paradise as they ascribe to the philosophy and literature of the land. One thing is missing and that one thing is that majority of them fail to understand that the kingdom of heaven or the paradise is a state of the mind, a figment of imagination beyond the sweep of the small minds nay the big minds.

As pointed out earlier, Yoruba religion is latitudinarian by nature. By this, we mean it embraces all the varying creeds and forms of religions, active or inactive. The long and short of it, cognate with its definition is that religion is a divine reverence for a divinity—monotheistically, and divinities or deities—polytheistically. Did Divinity Orunmila divine/foresee the coming of foreign religions to Yoruba country? Yes, he did foresee or divine the danger of the foreign religions in Yoruba land. That is why he said the following: "Yoruba spirituality is celestial and reverential. However, it is being adulterated and made fragile by the foreign religions. The sole weapon and tool needed to protect the fragile heritage is to intensify worshipping it every day without allowing the imported religions to consume it." The spiritual life of the Yoruba people depends on the calm strength of relation to Olodumare, highlighting three pillars, otherwise referred to as the religious or theological virtues—faith, hope and charity of love. For in Yoruba land, every household, every person believes in religion and the tantalizing paradise that awaits him or her under the vault of heaven. By way of a brief and narrow definition, religion is a divine reverence for our divinities or deities. By way of a long and broader definition, religion is a specific system often involving a code of ethics and philosophy.

The Yoruba Book of Enlightenment always reminds every scion in the land the do's and the don'ts as contained in religion and philosophy. It lets him or her know how his other latitudinarian ancestors/pedigrees were loved and guided by Creator-Philosopher Olodumare, the Oversoul. It is right to say that they have been able to separate their religion from mentalism. Mentalism may be antecedent to religion; however, it is religion whose homilies, divinations, rituals and practices lead to the definition of the holy city of Ile-Ife which provides a place of worship for all the ancestors or the pedigrees in the land. While mentalism, on many occasions, has nothing to philosophize about, on reaching the last chapter of its act of reasoning, religion always has something to preach and *ifamize* (my usage of ifa as a verb) even if it has reached the last chapter of its sacredness. Pushing overboard any vestiges of sacrilege, it may be correct to say that most Yoruba today have committed some degree of apostasy. But it is thrilling to see that many who have been trapped in apostasy are coming back home to where they belong. Some of them have begun to build shrines and temples, soon to be compared to the mega churches and the mega mosques. They have realized, though belated but quite redeemable that Ifa-Ife, the Book of Knowledge or the Book of Enlightenment, the autochthonous religion of the Yoruba people, one of the world religions, should not and must not play second fiddle to the imported religions in spite of the money derived from those foreign religions, dovetailing with brainwashing. In this day and age, in which mankind is relishing the fresh fruits of enlightenment: in this twenty-first century, the Yoruba society is waking up from its decades of slumbers. It is envisaged that the adherents of Yoruba religion would soon build their holy site, possibly in Ile-Ife, which this author has invariably designated as the holy city. The adherents would find it easy to travel to the holy city of Ile-Ife and perform their ablutions, while experiencing spiritual awakening and wellness, instead of travelling to another holy site which is not holier than their own holy land. Recognizing this is tantamount to recognizing the fact that Creator-Philosopher Olodumare is everywhere, listening and answering prayers everywhere. The Yoruba people do not need to spend thousands of Naira to travel to another country for the sake of holiness and salvation. Their Olodumare-given salvation is right on their palms! If they cannot visualize this, they should consult Divinity-Philosopher Orunmila, the father and the cultivator of Ifa-Ife Divination. As mentioned and highlighted on page 64 of Yoruba Idealism, published in 2022, when it comes to the practice of religion, Yoruba land is second to none in Africa.

For a long time, the adherents and the peddlers of foreign religions have one big fear. It is the fear of losing membership of their various houses of worship. This is why their leaders have taken to pooh-poohing the autochthonous religion of the land—the Ifa-Ife Divination. They often brag that they would be the sole souls who would be given visas to the tantalizing paradise, while the indigenous and lovers of the Ifa-Ife Divination would be denied visas to the same tantalizing paradise, the throne of Grace. What an untied bag of gimmicks! As the gimmicks are leaping out of the untied bag like the frogs, the leaders and the adherents of the foreign regions changed their lies to white lies, blaming the slave masters as well as the colonizers for not telling them the truth(that the Old Testament is likened to Ifa-Ifa folkways) the absolute truth, that religion, by way of definition, is the gathering or the fellowship of people who want to pray in unity to Creator-Philosopher Olodumare for their spiritual uprightness and wellness, while the purity or the contriteness of the heart is the sole salvation. Would Ifa-Ife worshippers ask the leaders of these foreign/imported religions to recuse themselves? The question is a rhetorical question with a difference, for it needs a crystal-clear/opalescent answer. That opalescent answer is a monosyllabic yes. Do we detect some elements of fanaticism in some of the imported regions? The answer cannot exist without a gargantuan, monosyllabic yes. (Yoruba Ronu by Hubert Ogunde. Yoruba are thinkers, not only are they thinkers, they are thinking thinkers). It shouldn't be this way. The autochthonous religion and the foreign religions should amicably coexist in the spirit of neighborliness, knowing that Creator-Philosopher God is not a religionist who selfishly dwells upon one particular religion.

If we should go by its world-wide and general definition, religion, as long as it is being practiced under a dwelling, is related to artwork and artwork is related to religion. As stated in *The Aesthetic and Moral Art of Wole Soyinka*, "art is present in all what we see and in all what we do not see but imagined"(Ogunyemi 2017, 175). As we cannot say that one art is better than the other, so also we cannot say that one religion is better than the other. However, there is more charity of faith, morality, love, honesty, honor, prudence, bravery, fortitude, justice and temperance in some religions than the others.

Religion and mentalism are like twins—the palm and the back of the palm or hand. They can as well be compared to a birth of twins—Taiwo and Kehinde. They have long entered a common plane of kinship in which their duality is like an analytical balance. The shrine is built in form of a cone. On the apex sits Creator-Philosopher Olodumare, pure in thought and noble in action, at the behest of who lies the fate or destiny, life and death of everyone and everything he creates. He is omnipresent, omniscient and omnipotent.

Below Creator-Philosopher Olodumare or Creator-Philosopher Olorun are his messengers, the deities, otherwise known as Orisas or the ancestors. They are many and may be up to 1700 in number. All of them are answerable to Divinity-Philosopher Orisanla who in turn confers with Creator-Philosopher Olodumare on a regular basis. Prior to theomachy, the deities enjoyed an excellent relationship with God. Whenever they bent their knees to worship, wherever they worshipped, God's Holy Spirit would abide with them. Soon after the theomachy, the earth was drawn further from heaven. Thus, Creator-Philosopher Olodumare distanced himself from the war-like theocrats. Though each one of them had God's stamp of dishonor stuck to his or her forehead, the Author of Life refused to destroy them, according to Divinity-Philosopher Orunmila, the brainchild of Odu Corpus. God had sent his children to multiply on the surface of the earth and is not going to destroy the world, for destroying the world is to destroy his own children who are both in his earthly and heavenly kingdoms. The works of Professors Bolaji Idowu and Wande Abimbola remain a vital bridge between the antiquity and the present.

Our ancestors have given us letter R, let us not disrespect by ignoring it because it leads to our indigenous religion that must change our views on the tantalizing paradise. In the twenty-first century, our ancestors/pedigrees have helped us in debunking so many gibberish things.

Literarily, literature has many layers and nuances of evocative emotions and enjoyments. That being said, let's pin upon *Myths and Weave.* Mythical and weave is the literary and artistic movement in Yoruba country in the late 9th century when every myth and weave was the will of Olorun/Olodumare (amuwa Olorun/Olodumare). It was the period of oral society when mononym was the order of the day. The mythical and non-mythical life of the Yoruba people depends on the calm strength of folklore that ultimately adds fullness to the meaning of life. We cannot but emphasize that the flavor and the piquancy of the Yoruba language began in the 1950s. The Yoruba language is enriched by the welding of the country patois and the learned urban words, phrases and idiomatic expressions.

Both the books of mentalism and religion, now known as Ifa-Ife, the Bible/Book of Knowledge of the land, or the Book of Enlightenment is the only oral monument or magnum opus that contains the chapter and verse of the literary traditions that started, shall we say, in the 1950s. Recognizing the fact that stress and rhythm are important in speaking and writing Yoruba, the literary history is divided into novel, drama and poetry. However, the main genre is poetry. In earlier times, the main genre which falls under poetry is ewi poetry. It is the kind of poetry which characterizes both moral and gauche behavior. An ewi poet can praise when he has something to praise. He can rebuke or satirize if he has something to rebuke or satirize. His poetic device is an endless repetition of metaphors, similes and proverbs. Ewi poetry is long and endless; long and endless like a vista that runs itself into the deep, only to resurface in the person of the nymph, locally known as "mamiwater." Is he not the ewi poet who warned the king of the wrath of the Infinite? It is the ewi poet who satirized the potentate who made love to the mamiwater when he refused to provide enough wells for his subjects. It is the ewi poet who poetized the rise and fall of the Oyo Empire. He, the ewi poet, lampooned the Oba who ordered the closure the School or the Guild of Arts in the holy city of Ile-Ife. The ewi poet is always on the top and he does not want to blow his top. An ewi person, regarded to have an old head on young shoulders, knows that literature has many layers of nuances and enjoyment.

From the Elders' reservoir of knowledge, an ewi poet is never created but born. In other words, a downright ewi poet has to be born. He cannot be created but born with the afflatus, that is with the divine creative impulse or inspiration. He cannot learn the art of ewi poetry without the afflatus. The ewi poet knows that his work belongs to the realm of literary art that regales upon artistic and cultural values, displaying the aesthetic of speech and language. The Elders and the keepers of traditions had reported of an ewi poet who foretold the birth of twins at a tender age of about nine years. He told the community that Taiwo (the last born of the twins), would build his low-ceilinged bungalow in seven days at the age of fourteen, while Kehinde, the elder of the two, would manage to build his in nine days at the same age. In short, he was trying to say that Taiwo was going to be stronger than Kehinde, contrary to the popular belief of the ancients.

No one believed the child-poet. Sooner than expected, a woman gave birth to twins. As prophesied, the twins began building their bungalows when they attained the age of fourteen each. Without further appositions, the last born built his low-ceilinged bungalow in nine days, while the first-born completed his in seven days. Practically, in all things that brought the twin brothers together, the younger was always found to be stronger and faster than the older. It was the first time people started wondering whether indeed Kehinde was the older of the two. Kehinde is the older of the two till today, according to the Yoruba cosmological beliefs, handed down to them by Divinity-Philosopher Oduduwa who was reported saying that the Elders and the keepers of traditions should not forget the logic of putting the youths before them in any journey they embarked upon. With the ancients, poetry and legends passed for history.

The younger brother started performing many wonderful feats. He could wrestle like a cat and acrobaticize like a rhesus. None could Kehinde perform. Although the Elders and the keepers of the traditions in the community agreed that Taiwo was a special phenomenon, one in a million, perhaps. It was a chastening experience for the ewi poet who witnessed the beginning and the happy end of his prophetic tale. He was eventually made the official "talking drum, the drum that interprets" the events in the the community." Two things had attributed and helped Taiwo here without the apology of ewi poet: one, he had quick wits. Two: he had old head upon his young shoulders.

The ewi poetry is like magic. Sometimes it astonishes. Sometimes it mystifies. Sometimes it carries one captive. Sometimes it is like scherzando. Sometimes it strengthens the imagination by sharpening its delicacies and enlarging its ranges, purviews and nuances. The ewi poetry is awesome, wondrous. It is largesse to the world, worldly. The Yoruba folklorists and mythicists cannot have enough of it.

Ewi poetry can act like a cure-all, an elixir or a panacea. Some researchers have likened it to Ramayana and Mahabharata. Ewi poetry it was, woven like a spider's web, and used as a bridge between heaven and earth. Ewi poetry has symbolized the making of *aso-oke,* the emergence of city-states, the rise and fall of kingdoms and empires. The lips of an Ewi poet portray a store house of proverbs, reminiscences, aphorisms and prophecies—his lips never dry, for he has quick wits. He is highly regarded so much that he is always made the chief of the palace minstrels and their lays. His wits and visions are profound. The demise of an ewi poet is like the death of a dwelling. Neglecting him is chaotic, anarchic and anomic.

As every work of literature has a generic context, so also it has its historical context. Below are the historical contexts into which Yoruba literature can be divided. Yoruba literature started during the era of theocracy. This was a period under the absolute government of Creator-Philosopher Olodumare, the Oversoul and his deities. The language is different from what is spoken today. This particular period started from the mythical day(s) of creation till about the eleventh century.

Medieval or Middle Age literature in Yoruba land belongs to the period between the eleventh and sixteenth centuries. This was the flowering genius of the Yoruba city-states. It also epitomized the height of artistic production. Many works of arts were produced so much that their artistic and literary values could not be assessed as the period was a preliterate or an oral culture.

The Yoruba Renaissance began between the 16th and 19th centuries. During this period, drama and novel joined poetry. And literary arts, that is stories and poetry that have meritorious values have commenced in earnest. (In full, literary arts are writings and stories that have artistic and cultural values which display the beauty/aesthetic of speech and language). Novel, the main generic division was already apparent. Poetry was always in the forefront, closely followed by drama. Dramatic performances, in tens and twenties: such as the Egungun and personality festivals could go on for days in compounds or pleasances, from village to village and from town to town.

The Renaissance period also saw a prolific production of myths, mythologies, legends and fairy tales. Literacy was sweeping across the land like the breath of Divinity-Philosopher Orisanla, for not only had the missionary Bible been translated in 1899, but also a standard orthography for the Yoruba language was re-alphabetized in 1842. A handful of "American/ Yoruba elite," on freeing themselves from the yoke of commercial slavery, had also come to the land, amongst who are Moore, Lawson, Coker, Johnson, Williams, Robinson, etc; including Bishop Samuel Ajayi Crowther, the first Anglican African Bishop, whose account was different from others as he was rescued before the slave ship he was bonded set sail from the Lagos harbor to the New World.

The first Yoruba novel, *Itan Emi Segilola*, by Isaac B. Thomas was published in July 1930. Adebayo Faleti and Chief J.F. Odunjo belong to the league of the first novelists in Yoruba land. The primary novelette (designed as a poetry book) to be published was *Iwe Kinni TiAwon Akewi*by Adetimikan Obasa, the editor of Yoruba News. The book was completed in 1896 but was not published in Ibadan until 1927.What could truly be said the first novel in Yoruba land, is entitled *ItanIgbes iAiye Mi*—The Life History of Me, published in 1929 by Isaac B. Thomas.

Modern Yoruba Literature can easily be said to have commenced in 1896, the very year Adetimkan Obasa completed his poetry novelette. Following *lwe Kinni TiAwon Akewi* was *llosiwaju Ero Mimo,* published in 1911 by Rev. David Hinderer. In 1934, Adetimkan Obasa brought out an Anthology entitled Iwe*Keji TiAwon Akewi.* In 1945, he published his third book, entitled Iwe*Keta TiAwon Akewi.*

Probably the most well-known creative writer between 1920s and 1930s was Kolawole Ajisafe. His works include novels and poetry, the most important of which is *Aiye Akamara,* published in 1921. This was followed by *Gbadebo Alake,* published in 1934.

The second novella, *lgbehin a dun,* by E.A. Akintan was published in Lagos in 1931. It is a tale about a maid who was orphaned in her tender age and later grew up to become a queen. In 1938, the first Yoruba classical novel was published. It is *Ogboju-Ode Ninu lgbo lrunmale*by D.O. Fagunwa. His fourth novel, *Irinkerindo* was produced in 1954. Following fagunwa's shoes was Adekanmi Oyedele whose novel *AiyeRee* was published in 1947.

From 1947 to 1948 when University of Ibadan was founded, producing its first batch of ivy writers in the late fifties, Yoruba literary works in poetry, folklore, drama and novel have established themselves on a historical map of creativity. From Amos Tutuola's *The Palm Wine Drinkard* (1952) to Wole Soyinka's *The Interpreters* (1965), the unique book that labored and then fetched him Noble Prize for Literature in 1986, it was evident that the Yoruba land had regained her lost house of oral literature. Let's rejoice in the good news that the oral literature has long been translated into visible letters, for one and all to consume with gusto, inspiring and promoting intellectual and artistic virtuosity. The train of that intellectual and artistic virtuosity was invariably full of artists of every description and never saw any derailment. It was obvious that the Yoruba nation was gradually and confidently falling in love with the sounds of reading, even writing. The nation has been fascinated by letters, books and the power of the word.

Yet the contemporary novelists whose names cannot but be mentioned are T.M. Aluko, Adebayo Faleti and Chief Folahan Odunjo. The three of them had their works published in 1963, 1964 and 1965, respectively. Of these three, T.M. Aluko is the most prolific. His first novel, One *Man,* One *Machete,* appeared in 1964.

From the village to the metropolis, and from the metropolis to the international arenas, three of the many traditionally trained playwrights vi-a-vis dramatists who have done Yoruba land honor are Hubert Ogunde, Duro Ladipo and Kolawole Ogunmola. They are traditionally trained because they do not make use of the Christian muse or the Muslim muse. They make use of Ifa-Ife muse. This is the distinctiveness of Yoruba *lfamization, and Yorubalogy*—the study of Yoruba works in the humanities—mentalism, religion, literature, history, sociology, anthropology, journalism and other human interests.

Speaking of honor; there is no soul without honor as long as you do not forget the kola nut of your culture, your mentalism, your literature, your religion. Honor is like Abiye. Dishonor is like Abiku, the antonym of Abiye, a mystical bête noire on the lips of every folklorist, redeeming the literary and cultural theory and the intellectual and artistic virtuosity.

The sole kola nut of honor which Gedu Ajanaka (see chapter Fourteen) last saw occurred when he unknowingly committed apostasy. Only Creator-Philosopher Olodumare could tell how often he had called him to defend himself before the Alta of Deism. Yet one honor can be more iridescent than the other. There is no hero-worshipping if the Yoruba land decides to give D.O. Fagunwa a national honor, while both the national and the international kola nut of honor goes to Wole Soyinka.

Talking about national honor, we may also recognize that Amos Tutuola is among the best in Yoruba land, for his Palm-wine Drinkard was included on the "Big Jubilee Read" list of 70 books selected by a panel of experts and announced by the BBC and the reading agency in April 2022 to celebrate Queen Elizabeth II's platinum jubilee in June 2022.

As though we are speaking in terms of an induction course, we must but remember, as noted earlier that the Yoruba alphabet is an immortal alphabet. It is not to be disrupted or altered. Any attempt to alter it will certainly lead to a hay of confusion to the Yoruba language, for the alphabet is a set of letters or symbols in a fixed order, used to represent the basic sounds of a language, in particular the set of letters from A to Y in the case of the Yoruba alphabet, and from A to Z in the case of the English alphabet.

Here is an extraordinary book we will need to ponder over. It is called an extraordinary book because it is diametrically different from published books, and can only be called a book by mononymous Ijapa, the folk hero and the fabled protagonist of antiquity of the Yoruba folktales. The core or the central point of our presentation is that there is no research project, academic or nonacademic that can be completed without a reference to Ijapa, the protagonist (invariably dallying with his medicine ball),and the father of Yoruba folklore. According to our keepers of traditions, the Thought Men and Women, Ijapa woke up one rainy morning, preceded by a gorgeous rainbow, telling his friend Fairy-bow that he wrote an extraordinary book during his dream, making use of object writing—cowries, shells and beads—in lieu of letters. The book which had two chapters was twenty-six pages long, including the prologue and the epilogue. The genre of the book was shrouded in a hay of confusion, likened to a pretty kettle of fish.

Chapter one was about the four elements—the Earth, the Water, the Air and the Fire. "I am the antiquity of the visible and the invisible universe, the genesis, without which nothing flourishes. To show you that I am the genesis of everything that ever be, I will now use my oracular authority to authorize or command a miracle out of the rainbow." No sooner had he said that than a red tongue of flame danced out of the rainbow, setting everywhere into iridescence.

"We can do the same. We can do the same," vociferated the Water, the Air and the Fire, simultaneously. The trio essayed to do likewise but there was no red tongue of flame emerging from the rainbow. Consequently, the Water, the Air and the Fire accepted the Earth as their senior, the genesis of the universe. Since then, it is opalescent evident to the trio that the Earth is antecedent to them.

Chapter two of the book is about the Rain-flowers. Rain-flowers are common between the rain forest and the savannah forest in Yoruba land. It is a fertile area for the farmers to sow their seeds of every description. The rain-flowers are deciduous colorful, flowering plants. They are called the rain-flowers because they are the beneficiaries of the rain and the dry seasons, according to the keepers of traditions.

Farmer Imokunle was a seasoned farmer who was lucky to have his subsistence farm in this fertile area of the country. One day, during the hush hours of the evening, he was going home having worked very hard and tired and thirty. On getting to the territory of the rain-flowers, he felt he was dehydrated and needed to drink otherwise he would die of dehydration. He began to supplicate for rain to fall so that he could have some drops of water to sip. Luckily for him, the bees who visited the rain-flowers on a regular basis had their habitat very close to the rain-flowers. They had heard Imokunle's supplication for rainwater. Out of compassion, dovetailing with the charity of love, they gave him some of the nectar they had collected from the rain-flowers. Farmer Imokunle tasted the nectar (the sweet liquid in flowers, collected by bees) and he became spirited and full of Pollyanna. His body had been revived from dehydration to hydration. He was very thankful to the bees, even to the rain-flowers.

Creative writing is the writing that is born out of imaginations, according to chapter thirteen below which is on Creative Writing. Creative writing can come out of dreams too. Ijapa's book of two chapters was born out of dreams. The question is: Is Ijapa's book, (a book in which he made use of object writing to complete) a book in the real sense? We may not be able to answer the rhetorical question until we have the opportunity again to interview the keepers of traditions, the Thought Men and Women.

Our ancestors have given us letter L, let us not romanticize it because it lets us yearn for the best in life, not only yearning for the best in life, as contained in Yoruba Idealism, published in 2022, it adds fullness to the meaning of life. That is what literature that has many layers and nuances of interest/enjoyment, does, dovetailing with other areas of the humanities.

PART ONE

MENTALISM (PHILOSOPHY)

Chapter One

The House of Ethics

Let us listen to what our research study has found out: The research study shows that philosophy and religion are ethically related. However, philosophy is antecedent to religion, according to Yoruba Philosophy and the Seeds of Enlightenment, published in 2018. It is philosophy that has designed and built a dwelling place, a bungalow, to be precise. Out of its love for ethical values, philosophy invites religion to stay in the bungalow. Again, out of its ethical values and the calm strength of love, philosophy urges religion to subscribe to love and homilies. Thus the beginning of religion inside the bungalow designed architecturally and built by philosophy.

Yoruba mentalism is a cultural or folk philosophy; recognizing ori—head as the definition of the body and the substrate to which all parts of the body are answerable. Ethically or morally, it seeks to explicate and point to the knowledge of the causes and nature of things affecting the corporeal and the spiritual universe, yearning/longing for wellness and organic happiness.

This chapter is one of the seven chapters of mentalism that sheds light on the fact that Yoruba philosophy has disentangled itself from all forms of setbacks and stirred away from the latent department to the department of lateral thinking. Those who have succeeded in moving away from the latent department to the department of lateral thinking can now be called the thinking thinkers, the creative thinkers or the lateral thinkers. It is a new dawn for lateral thinking has taken the center stage. It is a new dawn in the age of enlightenment.

As made elucidated supra, the house of ethics are, or simply put, the codes of morality in Yoruba land, which are very high and precious, cannot stand without mentalism and humanism. For mentalism, the kingdom of thought and the kingdom of reason is the theory that the physical and the psychological phenomena are ultimately only explicable in terms of a creative and interpretative mind. In its concinnity and proximity to the house of ethics, humanism defines itself as a philosophical and ethical outlook or stance that emphasizes the value and the divine love of (milk of human kindness) human beings, individually and collectively.

The house of ethics in Yoruba land is as old as the holy city of Ile-Ife. In other words, the Yoruba people have known ethics since the creation myth of the world. From their divinities, they have learnt that ethics is a branch of philosophy in which the society evaluates a particular course of moral actions. They have realized that ethics is a system of moral principles. As a matter of course, they are convinced that ethics deals roundly with what is morally good and bad, right and wrong.

Yoruba land has always been a polytheistic society. They believe in or worship more than one deity. All their deities, the Orisas or the divinity-philosophers are answerable to the supreme Deity who is Creator-Philosopher Olodumare. This makes them to be described as polytheistic at the bottom and monotheistic at the top which represents the head, the definition of the body. They believe their do's and don'ts come from Creator-Philosopher Olodumare via the intermediary gods in the menology of polytheism. Therefore, their concept of Creator-Philosopher God has every chapter and verse to perpetuate what is taken to be the norm of morality. Morality is therefore both the taproot and the fruit of religion. The two are inseparable. And no one attempts to separate them.

Good and bad, right and wrong are like a tabernacle with two front doors. While good and bad share the same entrance, right and wrong must go through the same door. No matter when and how they labor to go in, the two pairs must meet each other in the middle of the tabernacle. They must meet at the center because the Creator is always theocentric. In Yoruba land, anyone born of woman must meet in the center, the altar. For, the Creator is the center, and in the center lies one's harvest, consequences of one's words and deeds. Because we cannot separate morality from religion, every Yoruba is a believer, if not now, at least in the old days. And because he is a believer, he is duty-bound to adhere to what the Author of Life sanctions to be good or bad, right or wrong.

We have seen that it is good to be happy, to be successful and so on. Also, we have noticed that every soul wants to bask in the Grace of Creator-Philosopher Olodumare. You want to grow old, you want to be safe, you want to ward off evils and overcome difficulties. These positive desires (not the opposites), are the good and right things every Yoruba person strives for. In order to be happy and prosperous, one is obliged to do the right thing because there are rewards for the good and punishments for the bad. One doesn't have to kill before he knows that killing is bad. Yoruba people say if you don't know what it is to be painful, put your fingers in a fire. There is always a requital for good or evil.

It is the same Author of Life who dispenses rewards for good and punishments for bad that encourages obedience, and repudiates disobedience. Therefore, morality demands that we obey the rules and regulations as laid down by the loving-kindness of Creator-Philosopher Olodumare, for the Yoruba people not only think of the present world they live in, they think very much also of the hereafter.

The most important feature of Yoruba ethics is not obedience, disobedience, reward or punishment. It is *lwa*(character). Noble character is the most important mirror of the body. It is the sun that shines, the moon that shimmers. It is that quality which distinguishes man from a brute. Noble character is the real God's image in man, the very sense why the Yoruba say "we are created in the image of Creator-Philosopher Olodumare." Noble character transcends anything man possesses on earth. Yoruba land builds its moral education upon noble character, for it is character which the Author of Life judges before one's soul could be consigned to him. To the Yoruba, man's wealth on earth depends on his character, hence Creator-Philosopher Olodumare stresses that character must be the primary content in the house of ethics.

Granted with the same mentalism and with the same logic, granted with the same passion and with the same purpose, undoubtedly, happiness is the future tense of life. During the course of his research, this author would reminiscence upon the major and the minor premises (with adequate chiaroscuro) and verbalize thusly: *Where is love without happiness? Where is happiness without tlove*? The following are the main constituents which lead to noble character; the constituents of happiness and the stock or the fund of wellness:

1. Abstinence from falsehood
2. Abstinence from wickedness
3. Abstinence from stealing or robbery
4. Telling the Truth is like a theatre with adequate chiaroscuro
5. Cultivating the spirit of kindness
6. Cultivating the spirit of hospitality
7. Abstinence from selfishness
8. Giving honor and due respect to old age
9. Protecting women as the better halves
10. Abstinence from hypocrisy
11. Chastity rather than un-chastity should be uplifted in womanhood.
12. Avoid treading the path of pride and dishonor.

The Yoruba House of Ethics is like a folkloric ethos. It is handed down from the Author of Life to the children, via the deities, the ancestors and the folk memories of the Elders. For generations, Yoruba, as a people, have not only adhered to the house of ethics (the embodiment of happiness), they have also offered the divine souls their hands of fellowship and the milk of human kindness, accentuated by esprit de corps. As catechized by the ancient ethicists:

Noble character makes it easy for a village to raise its children
Never withers, the afrormosia planted by a noble character.
Like a torch, it lights the lives of the children, lighting the world.

Iwaniesin; Character is a religion. In an apt definition, morality is the taproot and fruit of religion, while character (iwa) is the faith associated with morality. That is, a religion forms a good character. It reflects in the attitudes and behaviors of believers. In sum, The House of Ethics lets us know that the Codes of Morality in Yoruba land are very high and precious and no one wants to fall under the attack of a bag-eyed behavior.

Courting Yoruba mentalism has emerged from a storehouse of success, cognate with progress; over dormancy and mediocre.

Chapter Two

The Aesthetic of Yoruba City-States

Ni atetekose (in the beginning), aesthetics was primarily an introvert cynosure. It was the age of i*walewa* (manners maketh man), when the inner beauty superimposed outward pulchritude. *lwalewa* is like *aso-oke*. It never tears, no matter how long you wear it. This is how Yoruba people have conceptualized their society for generations. And even today, the paradigm shift is minimal, especially in the country. As introvert aesthetics was the most salient characteristic of a woman of culture, so also her ethnic marks and tattoos were the most salient visual memories of the hey-day of city-states. In a stress and rhythm, the ancients and the contemporaries will acquiesce that aesthetics is the philosophy of beautiful things, especially arts. They may be reluctant to agree to the saying that of all the aesthetic artworks on the surface of the earth under the vault of heaven, Yoruba city-states are the most beautiful, simply because it was during one of the heights of the Yoruba classic art productions.

With the same perception and with the same logic, it is a new dawn, for Yoruba philosophy has stirred away from the latent department to the department of lateral thinking. Those who are benefiting from this new dawn of enlightenment will now be known as the thinking thinkers, the creative thinkers or the lateral thinkers.

As most historians will acquiesce, Yoruba land had experienced three major epochs that extended from oral to written culture. The first epoch was the time of gods and goddesses in which they had the propensities of moving between heaven and earth. The earth was not far from heaven, so the trip between one and the other was a matter of a wink.

The second stage came when theocracy metamorphosed into kingdoms and the land was garbed in a paramount administration. The third stage was chaotic and disoriented. It was a period of commercial slavery, followed by colonization by the middle of the nineteenth century.

Of these three epochs, the most remarkable occurred during the formation of Ife kingdom. It was the time aesthetics became both introvert and extrovert. Scholars regarded it as a cultural aesthetics. First, it was Ile-Ife the cultural capital, which enjoyed absolute statehood. Then other small-sized which enjoyed absolute statehood, followed one by one. These are Ogbomosho, Oyo, Owo, Ijebu, Ketu, Abeokuta, Oshogbo, Akure and Benin. They all enjoyed the spirit of autonomy, characteristic of city-states. Most of them relished fruits of prosperity between the eleventh century and the twelve century.

As the kingdoms prospered, so also poetry prospered. We were told that some of the epic poets used Object Writing (cypher) in their expressions and communications. Poetry, weaving, building, smithing, sculpturing, pottering, carving, carpentry, painting, wrestling, ayo-pastime, divination and hunting added pomp and pageantry to the aesthetics of the palaces of the city-states.

Ile-Ife, the marvel of wonder, the sacred city, the military, the cultural and the administrative headquarters of the land was regarded, reverently, as a god-send by other monarchs. The kingdom enjoyed a protagonist status, accentuated by the voice of Oni which was likened to the voice of Divinity-Philosopher Oduduwa. To buttress up his spiritual authority, Oni encouraged all forms of naturalistic works. And sooner than expected, it was seen that only the best sculptures could and must emerge from the holy city of Ile-Ife. The best sculptures did emerge from the kingdom. Not in hushed tones but in the crystal-clear tones, people would say, let's go and discover the lofty ideals and behold the jewels of knowledge in the crown of knowledge.

Sadly enough, there were occasional bloody clashes that threatened to pull back the hands of the dial. In spite of the gory clashes, the cultural aesthetics remained a cornerstone, irreversible. Its mentalism seated in the same board of divination with ethics, etiquette, punctilio, punctiliousness, cosmogony and cosmology.

If there is anything worth remembering during the reign of kings and queens, that phenomenon should be a conte of how a hunter became a royal mask-carver. As related by my grandfather, in the 1960's, the hunter's name was Oloko, living in Gbaguda, an outskirt on the imperial city of Oyo. He had gone on a hunting expedition and the expedition had been successful. But as he readied to go home, the rain started. It was a downpour. Rivers and lakes in the low-lying parts of the community had overflowed their banks.

Like a valorous hunter, basking in the calm strength of bravery, he asked Divinity-Philosopher Ogun to clear the way for him, after which he selected a fordable place in the pool and started wading. While wading, he looked into the pool. To his surprise, he saw Oni's face, as though it were in a mirror. On getting home, he began to ponder over a face he had seen only one. Weeks later, having asked Divinity-Philosopher Ogun to clear the way for him, he succeeded in carving a beauteous royal mask, a paragon of adoration, the very likeness of Oni's countenance.

Consequently, he went to Oni's palace. Having related his story, he dipped his hand into his bag, made of leopard's skin and surprised the king with his facial image. The monarch was not only flushed with delight but was also transfixed with shilly-shally. In the presence of the king-makers, he told Oloko that if he would let him have the mask, he would do for him whatever his heart desired.

Not knowing exactly what to say, the hunter begged leave of himself, promising the king that he would come back after two days. On getting home, he quickly sought Alafin's advice. Alafin made no bones to advise the hunter/carver that he should ask Oni to make Oyo kingdom senior to the kingdom of Ile-Ife.

Two days later, when the shadows were lengthening and the chicks were preparing to roost, Oloko (resplendent in his agbada) arrived at the palace of Oni. The potentate was glad to see him again, portraying himself as a connoisseur of naturalism. Without wasting time, Oloko told him that he desired no cowries or titles but prayed the king to make Oyo kingdom senior to the kingdom of Ile-Ife. Without a scruple, the king acquiesced, while the king-makers displayed their protest. Thus, Oyo assumed seniority over Ile-Ife in the seventeenth century, ere that seniority was reverted to Ile-Ife later in the century.

The only thoroughfare was said to be between the holy city of Ife-Ife and the imperial city of Oyo. Other paths were generally narrow but beautifully kept in the vicinities of the palace. How were the city-states built? They were built in concentric circles with the palaces in the centers. The center was a cluster of houses. A beehive of activities was the order of the day.

The king's palace was so important that its grounds occupied an extensive area of land. This was typical of Ile-Ife. Opposite the palace, was the city's most popular market. The joint location of the palace and the market in the center was, according to Bayo Ojo, (personal communication, 1987) "a rule without exception, hence the term Oloja was used as a generic term or title of a chief ruler of a town to be the king or Bale." From the center, the streets would diverge on smaller towns, villages and camps which were the dependencies. It was classic watching performers pouring into the center during a festival. Common was a panoramic rainbow of colors, a fascinating kaleidoscope of contrasts, eyeful, delightful; and the king and the king-makers, acknowledging and beaming with satisfaction. Again, *iwalewa,* was the metaphor that cosseted both visual and un-visual arts and crafts, the likes that typified both the interior and exterior city-states of Ile-Ife and old Oyo.

At the height of its glory, Oyo Empire, the shape of a cone, spread to Dahomey in the west and to Benin River in the east. In 1825, Hugh Clapperton, referring to the vicinity of the palace said that the ground palace was about one square mile, having two large parks, one in the front and another facing the north.

Both Oyo and Ile-Ife palaces were ornaments to city-states. The palaces were a museum of ornaments such as vases, masks, statuettes, calabashes, gourds and pieces of china, curios, as well as *aso-oke.* Some writers did suggest that Ile-Ife did have its own art school. If aesthetics goes by persons who appreciate qualities in arts, and the arts so appreciated, therefore the arts and crafts in ancient Ile-Ife could easily confirm that there was an undocumented art school in the kingdom between 950 and 1839, the aestheticism of which was epitomized and projected by old Oyo's artistry between 1698 and 1839.

As there is no perfection in a story told from different perspectives, so also there is no perfection in any oral narrative. Written documents have therefore become the sight, the hearing, the touch and the speech of our time. The following is both the oral and written chronologies of Yoruba land:

Circa twelfth century, Ifamas changed to Christmas.

From 950–1698: The rise of Kingdoms in Yoruba land.

From 1698–1839: The span of Old Oyo Empire.

From 1893–1960: The Yoruba land was under colonization.

From 1960 to 2007: The Yoruba land first enjoyed the civilian rule. Then gripped by the military hiccups, rescued in 2007 when the civilian rule, democratically continues, unbroken.

It must be noted that the fall of the Oyo Empire was not as a result of its weakness, militarily, rather it was because the Alafin was too complacent. Added to this is the fact that he did not know how large his armies were, and how defenselessly big his Empire was. Successes and failures are antonyms. This is why they can transpose at anytime. Let's hop from the city-states of remote antiquities to the skyscrapers. From remote antiquity to the contemporary, Yoruba land is still a land of kings. In the late 1940s three city-states came into being in what is today known as the "Atlantic Yoruba." They are Ayetoro, Ugbonla and Zion-Ipepe. Of these three, Ayetoro was the most dynamic and the most prosperous. It had its own schools, economic base, police and hydro-electric power. Visiting Ayetoro in the 1950s, a District Officer was reported saying, "From what I've seen, these people are excellent administrators. They don't need a foreign ruler."

Their status quo was to attain some kind of spiritual sublimity, next to God. Prayers were their primary means of cure-all. To the Atlantic Yoruba, the city-states were like *Sasarawa*in that they were solely self-reliant, self-supporting and self-sufficient, so also were they born out of prophecies. The only things they lacked were dependencies. The only time they came in contact with the government was the time of paying their taxes: the only time the government seemed to envy their status symbols, work ethic and qualities of life.

One person the Yoruba people dare not forget is Chief Obafemi Awolowo, who was the leader and first premier of the Yoruba land before and after independence in 1960. His egalitarian policies led to the introduction of free primary school education. He founded Tribune, the first English newspaper and encouraged the establishment of Yoruba newspapers. To his credit also goes the founding in Ibadan in 1956 the first African Broadcasting House.

An icon whose hat needs tassels is Wole Soyinka, Noble Prize Winner for Literature in 1986. He has not only fought for human rights and meritocracies in Nigeria, he has also fought for the "kola nuts of justice" in Africa, and amongst Africans in Diaspora.

Although other areas such as Ekiti, Egbado, Ijebu, Ketu, Ondo, Owo and Igbomina do claim status to city-states, the two city-states of substance between 950 and 1839 were Ile-Ife and Old Oyo. Oyo, having gained prominence over Ile-Ife, became a wealthy sovereign state like ancient Athens, Bremen, Florence, Genoa, Ghana, Hamburg and Sparta. Oyo, we were told, prospered not only because of its military might but also as a result of its excellent administration, the genius of which persists till today in Yoruba land of about 27 million. Its ability to change itself, uninterrupted, from a kingdom to an empire, is probably second to none in the history of ancient city-states.

With a charity of love, unity and diligence amongst the artists, especially the terracotta artists, it is correct to expound that the aesthetics of Yoruba city-states could not have been exquisite, splendid, wondrous, and magnificent and a sight for the gods without the aesthetic work of the artists. For art which is aesthetic, is made for life's sake, and not for art's sake.

Courting Yoruba mentalism is a push for the league of enlightenment where intellectuals and scholars will hug, discourse, reflect and then recognize Yoruba philosophy as a fund of common sense.

Chapter Three

The Facts, Fictions and Feelings of Queen Moremi Ajasoro

While regaling on the Yoruba nine cardinal virtues (love, morality, honor, honesty, temperance, justice, bravery, prudence and fortitude), we may find it necessary to assume that here is a new dawn, for Yoruba mentalism has stirred away from the latent department to the department of lateral thinking. Those who have succeeded in stirring away from the latent department deserve to be called thinking thinkers, creative thinkers or lateral thinkers.

The new dawn of enlightenment will reflect upon Moremi Ajasoro. The place of Queen Moremi Ajasoro in the history of Yoruba land is tremulous, surprisingly shaken like trees and willows in a hot-tempered tempest because it is thinly portrayed. While quite a number of historians, anthropologists and writers want to efface her name from both oral and written antecedents of her land, a few who sympathize with her phenomenal deeds and ethical values want to martyrize and iconize her, metaphorically. With stress and rhythm, she is an idealism in the body of Yoruba cultural/folk philosophy.

According to the oral history, Queen Moremi was born and bred in the holy city of Ile-Ife during the second half of the fourteenth century. She was married to Ajasoro, one of the prominent artists who belonged to the Ile-Ife School (Clan) of Artists and Sculptors, between fourteenth and fifteenth centuries. Her time was the second stage of cultural aesthetics in Ife during which the artists and sculptors reached the acme of their professions. She was the first woman to dally with the idea of equality between men and women. One of her remarkable achievements was that she succeeded in asking the Oba to allow women to officiate when worshiping certain deities, especially goddesses. This among other achievements and contributions to the land made her legend a medley of facts, fictions and feelings.

Ten of her favorite philosophical aphorisms are as follows:

(a) Ori (head) is the definition of the body, the substrate unto which other parts of the body are answerable.

(b) A sound sleep presupposes a mind at rest.

(c)A vista or path without obstacles leads nowhere.

(d) If you don't build your dreams, someone else will hire you to build theirs.

(e) Yoruba philosophy is a cultural/folk philosophy explicating and pointing to the knowledge of the causes and the nature of things affecting the corporeal and the spiritual universe, cognate with wellness and organic happiness.

(f) A cultural/folk philosophy is the cultural/folk philosophy of a people, depicting their cardinal virtues—love, morality, temperance, honesty, honor, bravery, justice, prudence and fortitude.

(g) Any lore that widens people's horizons and presents food for thought is the beginning of philosophy.

(h) In Yoruba land, there are many talking drummers, but it is not given to anyone to play all of them alone.

(i) It is not enough to preserve what we already have; we must try to create what we do not have.

(j) Yoruba idealism in Yoruba country and for the Yoruba people equates with the ideal purpose of life: the search for the meaning of life and the yearning for the best in life.

Symbolically, the three "fs" are a triplicity, forming what is said to be her nous and cultural ego upon which she built her motivations. In her perspective, there must be a fact before a feeling can be gestated, a genuine feeling which touches other senses of the corporeal. Facts and feelings must team together before fictions can emerge and become figments of imaginations. Moreover, facts and feelings are representative of the indispensable Mother Nature, as Queen Moremi is representative of muliebrity.

What an oral story loses in terms of narration is what is gained through sound-power by which the story is told. In other words, the sound and the punch line of a story are felt and enchanting only when a story is narrated aloud, not by reading it silently. The life history of Moremi is a merry-go-round of facts, fictions and feelings because there is no written record to support her life time. It is a fact because her history is constantly on the lips of the lfe citizens, and because the folk memory cannot do without her. It is a fiction because there is no written evidence to support her successes and failures, her days of happiness and her nights of sorrows. It is a feeling in that putting ourselves in her position, we could visualize her charm, her charisma and her character as a woman of the world, bearing sway over her triple personality.

Before we hasten to implore Divinity-Philosopher Ogun to clear the road for us, we may want to remember that there is always more than one road that leads to a market, either Oba's market or a "general market" for the people across the board. Retrospectively, there is *nothing* that holds Ifa-Ife Diviners accountable. *Nothing,* except that it failed to have written down its record of events, record that could have served as a locus classicus or magnum opus on Ifelogy as well as on a woman who some lips referred to as *mamilove,* as against *mamiwater.* Today, what are its limitations? They are probably many. Ifa-Ife, the Bible, the Book of Enlightenment still declines to tell us the birthstone of Moremi Ajasoro even if Divinity-Philosopher Ogun is more than ready to clear the road for us. Ifa-Ife, Divinity-Philosopher Orunmila's brainchild, will do scholars and discourses a great deal of good if only it sheds light on the parental background of Queen Moremi. Or, at least, to expatiate on both the higher and the lower criticisms of Ifa and *Ifamas.* No one but Ifa-Ife is in the position to bear a hand.

As per Bolaji Idowu (1962), Moremi, a woman of striking loveliness, saved Ile-Ife from defeat by Igbo warriors. The story was told of how Ife, for some reason, was plunged into a historical crisis. Using her position as a spokeswoman, Moremi volunteered to find out why defeat was always handed down to Ife warriors every time they encountered their enemies. There could be a ruse somewhere, she mused.

Like an Amazon, she stood position with the frontline troops and allowed herself to be captured by Igbo fighters. Before her capture, she made a vow with Esinmirin, a river goddess, saying she would make her a choicest offering if only she and her people could put the kibosh on Igbo menace and be victorious. Having been captured, she was made the wife of Oba of Igbo. From that vantage position, she learnt the do's and don'ts of Igbo army. Moons later, she escaped to Ile-Ife and consequently told Ife army what to do whenever the enemies menaced their territory again.

After a brief spell characterized by downpours, the Igbo warriors attacked Ile-Ife again, this time more determinedly than ever, partly because they feared that Queen Moremi had exposed the trick of swelling their numbers by displaying dummies, the upshot of their previous victories. But no sooner they advanced, attacked than they were repulsed by Ife infantries. Within hours, Ife territories were cleared of the armed rebels and declared safe. When the heroine's gallant role was reviewed by the king, she was made a member of the royal house and presented with a caparisoned hobbyhorse as a symbol for her heroic and charmed life. Being a member of the royal house did help to boost her public spirit.

On going back to the water goddess to fulfill her covenant, the water goddess told her the only one offering she needed from her was her only begotten son, Oluorogbo. With her eyes filled with tears, she turned back, went home and brought her son (who was a teenager by then) to Esinmirin. Thus, she lost her only begotten son for saving Ile Ife. "If she had not rendered her son to Esinmirin, Ile-Ife could have perished together with her and Oluorogbo," said the Elders and keepers of traditions. Following every twist and turn of the long and short of the story, Professor Idowu perorated by saying that Oluorogbo had unconditional passage to heaven. This might not ring a bell in that everyone who passed away in Yorubaland went to heaven, anyway, no matter whether it is a good or a bad heaven.

Let us now hop from the first version of the story to the second. Like the first version, the second version of the story has no written account to back it up. This is how it was summarized by Tai Bola (personal communication, 1963). There was once a beloved king in Ile-Ife. He was beloved so much that every woman in the city dreamed of being his princess. He reigned peacefully and died peacefully. Because he was so beloved during his life time, the artists and sculptors carved an effigy in his very life-size and then installed the effigy in one of his rooms in the palace, creating the impression that he was still alive and kicking. Without suspecting any foul play, the Chiefs, the king-makers, the equerries and the public paid homage to the king-dummy. After a while, the deception was exposed. Angered by the fact that he had waited too long before he was coroneted, the next king in line rounded up the artists and sculptors and ordered a near-wholesale slaughter of them. About two or three managed to escape. Moremi's husband, Ajasoro, was among those killed in the pogrom. Those who managed to escape set up a camp called Igbo, on the outskirts of Ile-Ife. Their family members soon joined them. That they attacked Ife at certain times, could not be ruled out, if only to demonstrate that it was wrong to massacre their colleagues.

Since the death of her husband, Queen Moremi had withdrawn into a cocoon of sadness and platitude. She was not happy. Happiness had eluded her like a house without a door. Like every woman in her days, she swallowed her bitterness and imbibed pages of her facts, fictions and feelings in harmony with her character. Despite her state of mourning, she remained a paragon of beauty. Because of her beauty, it seemed as though she had conquered her inward pain and man-made bereavement. Many men believed that a paragon of beauty should have no cause to be sorrowful and broken. That was not altogether the case with Queen Moremi.

In order to live above her dole, caused by the untimely death of her husband, she took to basket-weaving as a pastime. Her peace of mind, as could have been expected, was intermittently interrupted by the town's suitors who were asking her hand in marriage. Every now and then, she would decline, telling them she was yet to hear her husband's voice from the dead. The following is an adaptation of a threnody that gives countenance to Moremi as a heroine.

I know what had happened to Ajasoro.
The ears in the town know what had happened
to my husband.
You can fill my pot
But you cannot feel my pulse.

King Oduduwa knows the absolute truth

Creator Philosopher Olodumare knows the absolute truth

Ifa-Ife, the Book of Enlightenment knows the absolute truth
I will wait and take my cue
From Ifa's ubiquitous eyes.

One may not be able to fill Moremian pot of valor but one may feel her pulse. One striking anachronism is that Moremian story is akin to that of Penelope, wife of Odyssey. The similarity may stop there although Yoruba hold Ife as the Eden of mankind. However, Penelope could not have been

Moremi and Odyssey could not have been the slain sculptor, Ajasoro. Yet, riding in the same tandem are the Greek and Yoruba epic odes, classically sung on special events or occasions.

After years of putting her suitors off, she disappointed them by telling them that her husband's voice had warned her never to marry again, adding that her husband was waiting for her to join him. Thus, she eventually found her peace buoyed by a happy imagination. At that time, Oluorogbo had come of age. As a matter of fact, that was her secondary pretext; meaning she would not get married until Oluorogbo was big enough to shift for himself, hoping her burden would be lighter by so doing.

Making a study of the past and present facts, we may not be too quick to believe that both narratives share the same shred of truth concerning Queen Moremi and what she stood for. They were all crucial in the life history of the Apple of Ife's eye. No one can eliminate the vestiges of myths and mythologies in oral culture, knowing full well that a mythology can be historical, religious, philosophical or poetic. Myths and mythologies were great sources of entertainments during the innocent and the oral culture of the world, worldly.

The scenario is a qualified one, still in the offing. And it is not known if one day a holiday would be declared to honor the Apple of Ife's eye for her achievements, her intrepidity, her ego ideal, her dreams, her love, her passion and purpose for Ife and the entire people of Yoruba land. The following is a whisper (nay a mental reservation) to the rulers of the Yoruba land:

No biographers, no one
has labored to elegize you
No one sings your ode to the core
National holiday far from
being earmarked for you.
An array of kismets
But your ubiquitous eyes
Gravid with gravitas and déjà vu behold
the sacrifice of you only issue
saving the matrix of mankind.
The hands ringing your name
The lips singing your historical odes
are but a few libation conscientiously
to Mother Earth, accepting the
propitiatory blood of your womb, Oluorogbo.

Some of her achievements are: She discouraged the ritual sacrifice of twins. By sacrificing her only begotten son, she thus saved Ife from subjugation and humiliation by lgbo infantrymen. She succeeded in asking the king to allow women to officiate when worshipping metronymic deities or ancestors/pedigrees. Hence she has been described as the first indigenous woman to advocate equal rights between men and women.

There are quite a number of nature worshippers in Ile-Ife who deify her up till today, due to her achievements, her milk of human kindness, her moral values and her savoir-faire. Some Elders and keepers of traditions did assert that slavery (domestic or commercial), could not have taken place during her days in Ile-Ife because her heart was bound to love and her soul was grafted into humanity. This is why some writers have likened her to Harriet Tubman (1821–1913), the first female Abolitionist. Because Harriet Tubman was born centuries after her, it will be more proper to infer that the latter dwelled in the regenerate conception of the former.

So also will it be more proper to infer that Chief Olufunmilayo Ransome-Kuti (1900–1978) dwelled in the heroine's regenerate conception. Deriving much of her wits and visions from Herbert Macaulay (1864–1946), founder of Nigeria's first political party, Chief Ransome-Kuti was the primary suffragist and the pragmatic champion on Women's Rights in recent history, thus advancing Women's Political and Philosophical School of Thoughts.

In contemporary Yoruba Culture and Women's School of Thought, their retrospectives are linked to the spirit of the mother of Ile-Ife as a result of her wit and wisdom, her passion for equity and her empathy, probably second to none in the history of edifying oral culture.

If and when the folk memory regarding Queen Moremi (her principles over expediencies) is revived and pedigreed, we will have done justice to cultural history, political and social constructions, from evolution to revolution.

Moremi's personal mentalism, cognate with pragmatism. She was a middle-aged woman, belonging to middle-class, lucky with middles course who recognized the importance of middle term. Without kvetching, she invariably did her level best, always paying her devoirs to her community, as expected of a true patriot.

Courting Yoruba mentalism evidences the fact, as it reaffirms the hypothesis and postulation that any lore that widens people's horizons and presents food for thought is the beginning of philosophy.

Chapter Four

The Ontological Passage

If we believe that 2 into the power of 3 equals 8, we are duty-bound to believe that Yoruba mentalism has stirred away from the latent department to the department of lateral thinking. Those who are benefiting from this new dawn of enlightenment will surely be called and addressed as the thinking thinkers, creative thinkers or lateral thinkers.

In all beliefs, culturally and philosophically, human beings are on a borrowed life. We are created on a borrowed passport, passing through a borrowed passage. And according to our elderly patriarchs and matriarchs, no human on dying has ever regretted his or her leaving this world. The long and short of this is that human beings are like birds of passage, searching hither and thither.

Cognizant of this belief, Divinity-Philosopher Orisanla created every human, making use of clay which he had borrowed from Creator-Philosopher Olodumare. Creator-Philosopher Olodumare had lent him the clay on the understanding that after a while, the clay would go back to the earth—where it belongs, and the soul to Creator-Philosopher Olodumare.

In Yoruba land, everyone is a seller. Everyone has something to sell even if there is no one ready to buy anything. In other words, the world is a market. Having bought enough, you have to go back to heaven where you are supposed to have enough repast, forever.

Everything done in Yoruba land is accounted for—starting from the day you can discern the right from the wrong. From the time you know that *orunn ni ile, ayel'ajo*—heaven is the eternal home, the world is simply a journey. In all facets of Yoruba life, the philosophies embody all the characteristics of a journey, from an imaginary to a real journey, short or long. The ontological passage or journey is a constant phenomenon, linking the world with heaven, linking the "here with the hereafter."

Believing in the life after death, the Yoruba have wrapped their names up in the past, the present and the future ontological passages. Every name has a meaning, punctiliously and reflectively and divinatorily chosen. As a matter of fact, a name is a book of philosophy. It must be able to interpret the world and why such a name is given, for a name is never given in a vacuum. A good name can ward off evils. While a propitious name can lead to a successful community, a failed name can be a portent in a society. While growing up, a child is supposed to learn the virtues of his or her name, as well as the virtues of an Elder. First, he looks forward whenever he falls down, as he approaches adulthood. An experienced mind will pause, look back and ask himself why he had fallen down but an inexperienced mind has no time to ask himself, let alone looking back. This is a narrative to bring home the cosmological difference between an Elder and a youth.

Kako has been hunting since he was twenty-five. His older son, Jaiye, aged 9, could also aim without missing his target. But his younger son, Bode, aged 5, didn't like the noise made by guns let alone carrying a gun and shooting.

One murky day, Kako changed into his hunting suit, carried both his hunting bag and horn and then his gun, and told Jaiye to follow him. Jaiye followed him, carrying his own hunting bag and a dagger. They set out. A few yards after their village, Abule, Kako asked his son to move to his front. In Abule, it is forbidden for a youth to walk behind an Elder while going outside the community.

Having walked a distance of about three kilometers, they came to a forked road. Both of them stood still, confused.

"Jaiye, my instinct tells me that we should take the right road."

"It is the traditional thing to do, dad. Didn't the Elders say that in the right lies the good while in the left lies the bad?"

"Yes, the Elders said so. But apart from good and bad, the right hand brings joys while anything that lies to the left hand brings sorrows. By all means, nothing stops me from stalking a quarry that decides to browse along a left path. As you know, my gun knows no right or left."

Soon after this, father and son took the right road. A few meters after the forked road, Kako was tripped and fell down. He stood up heavily and increased his paces. A few minutes later, he was tripped and fell down again. Altogether, he fell down three times, but none of the falls bothered him. A few meters before they entered the hunting ground, Kako began to sing thus:

Isubu agba, ogbon lo je fun omode Isubu agba, ogbon lo je fun
omode Isub uagba, ogbon lo je fun omode
Eran pipa l'oko, ogbon lo je fun omode
Olodumare je kiari eran pa l'oni (ase)
It's wisdom for a youth whenever an Elder trips up and falls
It's wisdom for a youth whenever an Elder trips up and falls
It's wisdom for a youth whenever an Elder trips up and falls
Hunting quarries is a thing of wisdom for a youth
May Olodumare let us find a quarry to kill today (ase)

Although Jaiye did not join his father in the singing, he did enjoy his father's drumming voice. On taking a right turn, they came to a second forked road. The area surrounding this forked road was very muddy. Kako stood still while Jaiye took a few steps forward and within the twinkling of an eye, he was tripped up and fell headlong. With a low shrill, he stood up with a frown. His head and hunting suit were covered with mud. The next thing he did was to pluck yam leaves and then started to clean himself with the leaves.

Still standing by the muddy forked road, Kako shook his head right and left and said, "How can a strong boy like you be tripped and fell down like a coconut?"

"Anyone can fall down at anytime." replied Jaiye.

"But when a boy like you falls down, do you look back or forward?"

"I look forward."

"This is typical of young people like you. Listen; when an Elder falls down, he looks back and then starts his journey. Do you know why he should look back first?"

"No, dad."

"He looks back first in order to determine the cause of his fall. This is one of the different ways between Elders and youths. And this is why we say, 'Elders are rational, youths are irrational.' But my grandfather used to put it in another way, 'Elders are wise, youths are foolish.' But I never think youths are foolish. Rather, I think they are tempestuous."

Having walked up and down the hunting ground, for almost three hours, both managed to spot a gazelle at the same time.

"Sh," said the father.

"Sh," said the son, and within a second, he fired and the next thing they saw was the crashing of the gazelle. It was dead before father and son rushed to where it lay. Because it was too heavy for Jaiye to carry, Kako decided to carry it in his hunting bag. A few minutes later, and seeing that the shadows were lengthening, they decided they should be going home. But as they headed toward the main road, came a downpour. By the time they reached the second forked road, they were waist-deep in water. Rivers and lakes in the low-lying parts of the community had overflowed their banks.

They did not stop wading neither did the downpour abate until about a kilometer before they reached Abule. Although they were drenched to the skin, they were happy; happy that their hunting expedition had been successful.

But when Mrs. Kako and Bode heard how the two hunters had been tripped and fallen down, they were sad. Both of them said the two hunters ought to have known that no one goes hunting let alone crossing a forked road without making a sacrifice to Esu, guardian and seer of the crossroads.

Unlike most cultures, it is the philosophical craving that leads to the religious shrines and groves in Yoruba land. It is the philosophy that builds its premise around synecdoche's; the premise from which the whole can reflect the part and the part, reflecting the whole. As their religion is not complete without the journey betwixt the earth and the heaven, so also their philosophy is not complete without Creator-Philosopher Olodumare and the ontological passages bifurcated and enriched with realities and imaginations.

Yoruba names are not only representative of philosophy, proverbs, peace, honor, love, wellness, milk of human kindness, royalty or bravery, they are equally representative of religion. But what the scholars and intellectuals are searching for is the lighthouse that will shed light upon the apotheosis; particularly on the hypothesis so that one could comprehend whether the ontological passage is a perpetual passage in which the dead is reincarnated as the hope and desire of most cultures. However, rite of passage—a significant event or ceremony in a person's life, belongs to the domain of religion. Yet another question, unanswered is whether the board of divination portrays Odu literary corpus as a vehicle of transcendence and enlightenment in the realm of religion or as cognition in the realm of mentalism. But as earlier stated, it is the mentalism that first poetized the days and nights prior to the vistas that led to the religion of the land. The board of divination can therefore assuredly be projected that both mentalism and religion (whose chapters and verse are under the auspices of Ifa-Ife Diviner) are at the behest of the Author of Life. However, and to whatever degree, it is the former which gives birth to the latter, according to Ifa-Ife Diviner and his Book of Enlightenment.

Courting Yoruba mentalism ascertains that the head (ori) is the definition of the body, the substrate unto which other parts of the body belong.

Chapter Five

The Spiritual Cognition of Ase

GRANTED THAT ORI (HEAD) is the definition of the body, the substrate unto which other parts of the body belong, granted that cognition is an act of knowing, perceiving or conceiving, a new era has come to stay, for Yoruba philosophy has stirred away from the latent department to the department of lateral thinking. Those who have succeeded in moving away from the latent department to the department of lateral thinking, stand to be known as the thinking thinkers, creative thinkers or lateral thinkers. It is a new dawn and everyone is expected to benefit from this novel dawn of enlightenment.

The power of perception, intuition and reasoning, and all the mental activities are embodied in the spiritual energy of man and ase, acting as his alter ego. Through no human can one possess immortal spirit except through Creator-Philosopher God, the inimitable Giver of all things. All things, all humans, created by God-made ase have spirits. While some creatures have mortal spirits, some are blessed with immortal spirits. From the oral to written literatures, man, created in the image of Creator-Philosopher Olodumare, has an immortal spirit as long as he can atone for any fault if and when he commits an impurity; for impurities will rob the spirit of its purities and the holy gourd.

Man reminisces, reviews, reveres and revels in the poetry of naturalness of everything he beholds, in everything he touches, in everything he perceives, feels and smells. He can do all these things because the spirit of Creator-Philosopher Olodumare abides in him. The good in the Creator makes him feel good.

The spirit of the Creator/Oversoul has always been with man since the creation of the world. When Creator-Philosopher Olorun created the world, he created it with the spirits of eternity and ase, the creative and psychic energy. Man can live as long as he wishes if only he cultivates love, faith, hope and charity and God's spirit will dwell in him forever. That man cannot be pure without God's spirit must be emphasized here. Man in his eternity, is an infinitesimal part of the image which is Creator's image.

Like Adam and Eve in the Good Book, the theocrats in the old Yoruba land had every opportunity to live next to their Creator. The life of the theocrats was supposed to be flowing with milk and honey; free from disease and physical death. But sooner than expected, they plunged into rivalry and from one impurity to another. First, it was nature worship. Then they indulged in the practices of slavery and from slavery to theomachy which eventually distanced them from God. They lost everything except their individualities. In his generosity and benignity, Divinity-Philosopher Orisanla gave ase to all his consanguineous colleagues and by so doing, he harvested Creator-Philosopher Olorun's flaying postscripts in his letters of immortality, as well as some unpleasant post positives.

Life has the character of unknown and the unknown has the character of life. A dream is life in sub-consciousness. Conversely, life is a dream in consciousness. Creator-Philosopher Olodumare gives life to everything that exists. Everything that exists has life. Man is the last to be created in everything that exists. There is a spiritual life and there is a material life. While a material life is devoid of a spirit in the image of God, the spiritual life is the fullness of eternity, holiness, omnipotence, omniscience and omnipresence. As every culture has experienced nature worship, so also every culture has experienced slavery. As theomachy yielded to divinity and the more spiritual benevolence of Tetragram, so will material spirit yield to the energy and propensity of spirituality and ase and their appetite for life.

Every day, something good and bad happens; you and I will agree. Everyday, a child is born. Every day, a child is dead; you and I will agree. Do we believe in eternity? Is believing in eternity the fountainhead of our happiness? Whether yes or no, there is nothing we could change, for the Creator had rightly created the world by means of ase. Like a quicksilver, is life. Those newborns are the returning spirits, while those who pass away are the departed spirits. Life is therefore a merry-go-round. It must take its course of nature; in accordance with ase. As often said; one generation goes, another generation comes. The philosophy of existence, of the world we live in, is simple if we take a moment to reflect upon why the Creator never dies, and why the world cannot be perished. The world cannot be perished because you and I are the salt of the earth under the vault of heaven, under the canopy of heavens which is analogous to the Creator-Philosopher Olodumare who never can die. Until recently, ase was regarded a creative force, an energy, capable of fulfilling the desires of every soul; a creative energy which can change yes to no, and no to yes. But today, researchers have found out that ase is not only a psychic energy or a creative power but also a womb which conveys all the cultural panoplies and imprints of the Yoruba land, ensuring kinship with Mother Earth. Ase is like a stamp which seals a contract between two parties, forged upon a philosophical and psychological anvil. To all intents and purposes, ase does not only seal a contract between two parties, forged upon a philosophical and psychological anvil of destiny, it also acts as a window of opportunity for whosoever desires more success than failure.

According to the Yoruba mythology, the soul is like a destiny, picked up on the way to the world. Hence the soul is greater than the mind. There will be no mind without a soul, as there will be no man without the Infinite. The soul, like the spirit, is immortal and because it is immortal, it cannot perish like the Infinite, even if it departs this physical world of ours.

From time to time, theorists do argue that the soul precedes the spirit in order of creation. This postulation holds no philosophical analysis other than the opposite of the eternal verities. First and foremost, the spirit. It is the soul that enters the spirit and not the other way round. A theory without ase stands to be without eternal verities; and other cognate postulations such as meta-psychological theories are distancing themselves. According to the oral theorists in Yoruba land, Creator-Philosopher Olodumare breathed life into the spirit (a figurine) as molded by Divinity-Philosopher Orisanla. So was the creation of human beings.

The philosophy of living is to live the best you can while you are *here,* or while you choose to be *there.* The idea of living *here* for as long as you desire is to consume the eternal ambrosia of spirituality, which can only be obtained fruitfully from meditations and prayers. Nothing can make one free from one's suffering and death without seeking the healing power of prayers and meditations, the offshoots of ase. If you want to live a pain-free life, if you want to live and get closest to the Author of Life, the surest thing to do is to bedeck yourself with prayers and meditations. All other things on earth may be polluted but prayers and meditations are not. The more you depend on prayers and meditations, the less your body, your soul and mind will depend on drugs and physicians and pharmacists. Praying and meditating will bring you closest to the Creator and to his Ark of Salvation. This view has been substantiated by the theological virtues on which every oral and written faith has built its foundation.

Man, created because man has a mission. Man departs either because he has accomplished his mission or he can no longer fulfill his mission.

> Knowledge gathered from ignorance is useless
> Any desire or plan without ase is doomed to failure
> Repast munched from impurities is perilous
> One born out of love faces discomfiture
> Cultivation of a spiritual love is the passport
> to wellness.

While meditating and praying, take cognizance of the following four elements which are indispensable to both your spiritual and corporeal wellness of ase:

> The Earth, no one exists without it
> The Water, no one exists without it
> The Air, no one exists without it
> The Fire, no one exists without it

No one has ever had the cause to be in ire with them. Human beings are the offshoots of their existence. It is the law of nature that they should account for our development, spiritually and physically. The spirit of the human body cannot be duplicated. It is either the spirit in the likeness of the Creator-Philosopher Olodumare or nothing at all. Spiritual cognition of ase does not support any scientific or philosophical cloning of any form or shape. Attempting the cloning of a human being is to attempt to tamper with ase which is indivisible.

The spiritual and therapeutic power of meditations and prayers will buttress up personality, dynamism, creative energy, creative spirit, clarity of vision, spiritual and corporeal wellness, unconditional love and rapport with the highest spirit which is Creator-Philosopher Olodumare and his ase, that dignifies him as the Author of Life, even Death.

Courting Yoruba mentalism validates the theory that Yoruba Idealism equates with the ideal purpose of life, the search for the meaning of life and the yearning for the best in life.

Chapter Six

Ifalogy And The Kola-nut of Peace

While giving countenance to head (ori), as the definition of the body, we must realize that Yoruba mentalism has broken down all the barriers in its way to recognition. On breaking down all those barriers, it has moved from the latent department to the department of lateral thinking. Those who have succeeded in moving from the latent department to the department of the lateral thinking will be known as the thinking thinkers, the creative thinkers or the lateral thinkers. It is a novel dawn of enlightenment and eclaircissement for one and all.

All the Holy Books in Africa, Asia, Europe, North and South America carry the rudiments of peace. They have in many kaleidoscopic respects a unique character among other books in the world. Aside from their sacredness, the Holy Books of worship have been able to feed the entire world with moral philosophy, intelligence, literature, history, wisdom, poetry and common sense and common weal, cognate with sensibilities. They have appealed to both young and old, expecting to relish the tantalizing paradise, the throne of Grace and the absolute bliss.

In Yoruba land, the foundation of a youth portrays the letters and the spirit of Ifa, while the health and peace of an Elder demonstrates his or her obeisance to the letters and spirit of the book of worship.

"I belong to a house of worshippers. We worship peace. We put peace between the pillar and post in our compound. Every day, we worship the illustrious phenomena of the universe. The Altar of Peace, everywhere in our house. But the greatest altar is the one sandwiched betwixt the pillar and the post." This is the description by Ojomo, a nature worshipper, of how Ifa-Ife was worshipped before any religion was imported to the land.

Wars are fought in order to have a shower of peace. People are enslaved because the slavers are looking for peace that could be thrust upon them by slavery. Churches, synagogues, temples, shrines and groves are erected because people intend to marry peace as a necessity or as a desideratum. Universities and international organizations are founded because they vow to search for peace in their constitutions.

Where is the peace, O Lord? Where is the peace, O Lord? Where is the peace you promise the earth? Open the door for me. Open the womb for me. Let me go. Let me go to the virginity of the glebe. There lies the peace. There I will find my peace. This is my soliloquy, versed in 1973 as I knelt before an altar in Europe.

The eternal city of Rome is no more because the world has left peace behind it. Our apparels are polluted because the earth is polluted. Because the earth is polluted, human-beings are equally polluted. What pollutes the earth, therefore pollutes the mind. Nonetheless, the earth breathes, but it stops breathing anytime it is fouled, the voice of the oracle. The good news is that it accepts our "unsuspecting propitiation" anytime we urinate on it.

Retrospectively, the Middle Age lived with abundant peace. They lived with abundant peace because they never polluted their world and we are not ashamed to refer to them in our discourses because we know they had peace of mind, the peace which we find elusive today.

A child, a year-old child told his parents that he was going back to the virginity of the earth. They asked him why. He said he could find no peace since he was born. The ecosystem was in disarray instead of being in rhythm, melody and harmony with Mother Nature. The air was foul and the people around him were hungry for peace of mind, he concluded. His parents begged him to stay but he declined, promising them he would be back as soon as the world could wear spiritual peace as against the material peace which is degenerative to the philosophy and psychology of the innermost.

Peace had long taken a catnap from the mind of the world. The world without peace of mind has been partitioned by a catenary bridge. To the past is the spiritual peace. To the present is the material peace. Because of this uncanny division, the earth suffers pollution in the hands of the present. There is no gainsaying the obvious that the Mother Earth is burdened. We have fouled our natural life-supporting system. Hence the center refuses to hold the much needed peace. We have been dispersed to the tree-branches because the polluted earth is not pleased with our super-highway behavior. The following is a legend born after the Yoruba land is faced with pollution toward the last quarter of the nineteenth century.

Once upon a time, there was a village called Mercury. It was built between two paramos. The valley village had a population of 5, oooo.

Mercury, to say the least, lacked some essential things. As a matter of fact, it boasted of nothing except water. It had abundant water supplies, majority of which were natural. It had many wells. It had many rivers. It had many fountains and water-falls. It had a lot of streams, brooks, anabranches and lakes.

One stigma; and it was a big one, which Mercury had was that every male in the village was bald like a vulture. Females were the only exceptions.

Males and females from other surrounding villages and towns (three villages and two towns), were scared to visit the bald village, for any males that visited the "barren village," as it was otherwise called, would be bald like the villagers themselves. Although females from other villages and towns were immune from the plague, they were nonetheless afraid to visit it.

Most of the young girls and women preferred to marry from the surrounding villages and towns. One young bride, during her bridal party, was asked to say one or two words about her happiest days. She said, "One of my happiest days is not to marry any of those bald men in Mercury." A joke had been cracked and the whole party was rocked by a thunderous laughter. Mercury boys and men had been made laughing stocks.

Not only the males in Mercury were bald, the birds, the animals—(drupeds and quadrupeds), the fishes, the trees and the hills were also bald. As the birds had no feathers, so also the animals were hairless. As the fishes had no scales, so also the trees had no leaves, and the hills devoid of trees and bushes. To other people from villages and towns, Mercury was a ghost town visited or imagined.

That the surrounding villages and towns were more beautiful than Mercury was as true as truth could be. They were richer too. Richer and beautiful, oh yes, but one important thing was missing in their lives. That vital thing was water. The surrounding villages and towns had no rivers, lakes and rain rarely fell. Their survival lay with Mercury. Without Mercury, they would all thirst to death.

In order to have water for their daily use, the surrounding inhabitants had to draw their daily use of water from Mercury.

The sole people who could draw water were girls and women. And they had been doing that for years – since the villages and towns came to live together as neighbors. Almost every hour, one would see them carrying their gourds, bowls, calabashes and pots of water, going to their respective villages and towns.

One late Sunday afternoon, when the hours of the daylight were ebbing away, and the shadows becoming longer, the females of the waterless and rainless villages and towns held an emergency meeting with their male counterparts. They demanded that their male counterparts assist them in fetching water from mercury. "Please help us, we are tired of doing the job alone," said the females, rather cathartically.

More than three men stood up at the same time, and simultaneously said, "No. No. This is not possible. We are the bread-winners. All we ask you to do is to fetch water so that we all have water to use. Remember that no male dares to go to Mercury without becoming as bald as Sahara Desert. You don't want to have bald husbands, do you?"

The women and girls stood and said in one voice that they needed no bald-heads as husbands. The meeting came to an end without an agreement on both sides.

A moon later, another meeting with the same agenda was convened. Again, males declined to fetch water. They reiterated that fetching water and firewood was cushy, and as easy as ABC.

Two months later, the third meeting was held. Like the first and the second, the meeting came to a close without making males agree to help their female counterparts.

During the fourth meeting, a male child was born in Mercury. His name was Ileya Goya. At the age of seven, he was considered a genius because he could tell orally all the family histories in Mercury and all the surrounding villages and towns.

One Saturday morning, when the sun was beginning to rise, Ileya Goya called all the Elders to a meeting. All the Elders were excited, waiting for the genius to open his mouth. When he did, he said that the reason why Mercury was bald was that Mother Nature was famished for homage and submission, adding that the Elders had forsaken their traditional duties to Mother Earth upon which they trod every day. "The land had been desecrated and must be propitiated," declared Ileya Goya.

The Elders knew what to do because the wisdom of the youth is no way to be compared to the wisdom of the Elders. Can a child be older than its living parents?

Seven days later, in a sweltering hot midday, the Elders in the company of the genius, milled to River Maku. Here each one of them dipped his head into the river, nine times. On coming out of the river, they kowtowed, also nine times.

Days after the appeasement, baldness disappeared from the life of Mercury, not without some pregnant constructions. The surrounding villages and towns, like Mercury, enjoyed a new era of happiness, peace (more spiritual than material) and prosperity. River Maku was renamed River Ileya Goya in honor of the infant prodigy who brought peace, abundance and life-essentials to one and all.

Children are the primary friends of the earth. They are the curators of the fruiting tree that grows on earth. Without them, there would be no peace, no future and other ingredient of life. Our researchers have shown that no study of any sort can prosper without a mind, a mind infused with peace.

Our homes, our communities, our societies are not looking for political peace. Nor can they derive peace from the science laboratories. Political peace is nothing but rhetorical pages of words, devoid of spiritual peace. The spin doctor spins political but rootless yarns. The Mother Earth spins peace yarns emblazoned with love.

According to Bill Graham, in his book, "World Aflame," published in 1964, the world will continue to be aflame until a spiritual mantra is able to put kibosh on the environmental pollution which is twisting the peace of our minds. Cleaning up is the ultimate solution. The meta-psychologists and psychotherapists can do little or nothing without cleaning up. Let's clean up our acts. The children will stop fretting and whining. The earth will stop hypnotizing our feet instead of imbuing them with ever-lasting peace. Let our children possess sound minds now that we are about to enter the year 2000, for a sound mind is a good health. A healthy people is a healthy community of males and females.

Ifalogy, the branch of theology concerning Ifa's values can hardly stand without the kola nut. In fact, it cannot stand without breaking the covenanted kinship. As there is a ground swell betwixt Christology and the Savior, so also there is a natural force between Ifalogy and the kola nut. Betwixt Ifalogy and the kola nut is a Gordian knot. Only peace is able to untie it. The bond between the two is like the bond betwixt a mother and her daughter. The onus of carrying the divinatory calabash of kola-nuts to the altar of peace rests with Ifalogy, always.

In a democratic society like ours, it is not the government which sheds light on the status quo but the media. This is why the media practitioners must join hands with moral philosophers, the psychologists and the natural healers in their search for a permanent peace, peace for everyone across the board. Must we be called children of the earth when peace is miles away? In order to have an everlasting peace, we must plan a spiritual seed. Its fruit shall be a balance of diet for our minds and souls; for a peaceful mind is a healthy house of happiness.

Courting Yoruba mentalism confirms that the Book of Enlightenment is antecedent to the autochthonous Yoruba religion.

Chapter Seven

What Comes After Six Is More Than Seven

IF WE SHOULD ALLOW our argument to be in line of our reason, and the line of our reason the pith of our argument, we will acquiesce that what comes after six is more than seven. This aphorism points to the fact that Yoruba mentalism has matured during many years of growing and has now taken its rightful place amongst the world philosophies. it has been able to accomplish this because it understands that learning is a cumulative process. Similarly, it has graduated from the latent department to the department of lateral thinking. As the world will be benefiting from its lateral thinking, it will be opalescent clear that it is a new dawn of enlightenment and everyone—students, faculty and the uncommon thinking thinkers. Yoruba land is a byword or a proverb for uncountable words; words bedecked with both earthly and heavenly Attic salt and wit. The virtuosity of a proverb resides in its virginity or virility. We may dare say that there will be no philosophy, religion or literature without a proverb, for the search for the truth, the meaning, the sensibility, the rationale and the Atticism in Yoruba culture dwells in its Attic wits.

The days and nights of an Elder are but marked with sayings. The mat upon which he sleeps is woven in the presence of "What Comes After Six Is More Than Seven." And the heaven he looks to is a starry abode of witty sayings. What he does or says is incomplete and insignificant without a proverb. This is why he always strengthens his words and deeds with proverbs. Of all the Attic wits in Yoruba land, the most important but less discussed is the title of this paper.

Why is it that "What Comes After Six Is More Than Seven" is the most important of all proverbs in Yoruba-land? One of the reasons is that "six" is the most conspicuous ordinal number. It (6) is also the most metaphorical cardinal number. It is the fulcrum between the first five and the last four digits. It can be transposed into nine at anytime. "Six" is the most propitious number in Yoruba alphabets. It is a number full of hopes for progress, success and accomplishments. The proverb denotes muliebrity or womanhood. It is everything that comes after it, yet everything that comes after it is more (six fold) than it. *Ohun to'nbe lehin mefa o ju meje lo:* its paraphrastic meaning goes thusly:

Whatever happens in Yoruba land is always less than whatever will happen in the future. The proverb is a store house of optimism. Hence the Yoruba will try seven or nine times before giving up any task or situation. Over the years, the Attic salt has become a household food for thought, not only among the Elders but also among the youngsters. Rightfully, the Ifa deities or philosophers have secured its place and others in the Bible, becoming the Yoruba Book of Proverbs. The book is an authority on Yoruba proverbs, aphorisms and maxims which help to strengthen all the words and deeds: words and deeds which when devoid of those witty sayings convey no substance upon which an Elder can interpret the future events in particular, and the present in general.

"What Comes After Six Is More Than Seven" helps us to know why the chameleon changes his color. Meticulous and circumspect is the chameleon because he (as one of the heroes of antiquity in the land) knows the meaning of the proverb. He knows the dos and don'ts of the land too. He had learnt practically everything due to his circumspection. Other animals did not like him for that. They were jealous of him by virtue of his meticulousness and circumspection. As related by Tai Bola in 1963, the chameleon did not acquire his ability to change his color overnight. He went through three stages of unsuspecting embarrassments.

The first one happened when the lion called the meeting of all quadrupeds. All the quadrupeds wore the color of the earth. Only the chameleon wore a green color. Because he wore a different color, he was asked to leave the meeting. He left by saying "What Comes After Six is More Than Seven."

His second embarrassment took place among amphibians headed by a horned crocodile. All except the chameleon wore beige color. Shortly before the meeting commenced, he was asked to leave. He left by saying "What Comes After Six Is More Than Seven." The third embarrassment occurred the very first time birds and animals decided to devise some means by which hunters would find it absolutely difficult to shoot them. The meeting was full to capacity, but no sooner the lizard entered the meeting and sat down than he was told he was not welcome, although he showed the organizers his invitation. Anyway, he left the gathering by saying "What Comes After Six Is More Than Seven."

He was upset to say the least. Three days later, he went to the Creator and prayed him to remove him from the surface of the earth. The Creator asked him the reason for such a weird request. He said he was a weirdo because he was never loved by either the bipeds or the quadrupeds as a result of his green color. The Creator then told him that henceforth he would give him the ability to change his color as he likes. Since that day, the chameleon possesses the ability to change his color. Flushed with joy and gratitude, he added the ability and capability to change his color to his virtues of meticulousness and circumspection.

On hearing how the chameleon was treated, Chief Kariju of Obade made him the first sacred quadruped in his chieftaincy. A hero and a sacred lizard, his life epitomized the interpretation of the aphorism. Stories such as this one help to conceptualize the unique department to which the Attic wit belongs.

Like a divination proverb, the saying sets aglow the human ambitions, putting the full moon on the face of the daring. Is it not an ambition on the lips of the child who says "Let the sun shine endlessly, never to set!"

What comes after six is more than
Happiness without a foundation
What comes after six is more than
Love without a vase of roses
What comes after six is more than
The body without a head (ori)
What comes after six is more than
Peace with a weather emblazoned with tranquility.
There are more than six seas to cross
There are more than six mounts to climb
There are more than six songs to sing
There are more than six journeys to make
There are more than six mouths to feed
There are more than six farms to finish
There are more than six poems to memorize.

This is what Adegoke (personal communication, 1987) said to his son in Ibadan in 1987. His son, on coming back home from the University of Ibadan (which is regarded as the intellectual colony among the academics, an ivy institution) told his father that he had read six authors and so he was a student-intellectual. His father knitted his brows, laughed and said, "What comes after your six books is inadequate to make you an intellectual."

The ambitious student has the right to call himself a student-intellectual and his father seemed not to have disagreed with him except that what comes after those six books is more than what the future holds for him. Certainly, he has to read more than six books if he wants to become an intellectual with a mark of genius on his face. There is no question about that.

Some researchers on Yoruba proverbs, aphorisms, adages and maxims have referred to the title of this paper as a cardinal proverb which carries the repertoire of futurists. Other authorities say its wide range of allusions and optimisms transcend any cultural barrier, reminiscent of Yoruba world-view. It is one of the few proverbs that replace world-weary with world-pleasing.

According to Adegoke, the proverb is all-purpose and multicultural because it can be used by any culture, anywhere in the world. Hardly can a keeper of traditions complete a paragraph without the use of a proverb. He went further to say that it is the only classic Attic salt in the entire Yoruba land when it comes to an "unfinished job" for an ambitious mind who wants to reach the top of his bent in life.

Courting Yoruba mentalism is the head of the table, the capstone printing the integer 99 that precedes 100, as *aso oke* precedes *aso adire.*

PART TWO

Religion

Chapter Eight

The Literary Significance of the Divinity-Philosophers

TAI BOLA (1898–1989), TUTOR, diviner, bucolic philosopher and member of Ogunyemi family, has once said that that everyone is a *sacrificer*, (offering sacrifices on a daily basis) inasmuch as we consume foods such as animals, birds, fishes, fruits, etc, to satisfy our hunger. "The choicest sacrifice used to be offered to Creator-Philosopher God in the days gone by but today everything is offered to man's stomach," he concluded, knitting his brows and folding his lips.

When the act of reasoning prevails, gods and goddesses are discoursed by philosophers, thence cometh the vagaries of human emotions, dissolving into their innards. Consequently, mentalism/philosophy flows like rivers to mythology, and mythology metamorphoses into mythography, and vice versa. Today's mythography cannot be matched with the past because today's genre of writing has banished traditional literature. One thing though which oral literature still has in common is the impalpability of the past which ironically is the *joie de vivre*. We still have a hen together with her spouse. Once, the Elders said the ancient writing was encoded from the scratching of the earth by a hen. Every scratch a hen makes on the surface of the earth has a letter, and every letter, a meaning, just as metaphysics whispers its composition in the ears of the moral philosophers.

In Anno Domini of 1960, I came across Elders asking the not-willing-to-learn students to watch the hens scratching the earth. After some forty minutes, they said that if the hens could write (scratch), the students could as well write. This is another sure-footed vista to mythopoeia.

Every ethnic group in the world has a number of gods. There is no society without a belief and believing is a major premise for having gods and goddesses. As there is no society without a belief, so also there is no society without mythology-religion. With about 1,700 patronymic and metronymic deities, Yoruba land will share the same apogee of syncretization with India and Greece as the lands having the largest numbers of gods and goddesses.

Yoruba gods and goddesses are numinous and numerous but there are only two of them who have direct bearing on the realm of letters. These are Divinity-Philosopher Orisanla and Divinity-Philosopher Ogun. Let's start with Divinity-Philosopher Orisanla, the image of Creator-Philosopher Olodumare on earth, the only one who has the chapter and verse to creation of the physical part of man, and the creation of the earth as well as the arrangement of its trappings. He is a toucher and finisher: a sculptor-divinity who has been given the authority to create as he chooses. Not only he is an improviser of [fa (the autochthonous Bible) with his white chalk, he also has the power to ennoble and make his worshipper and believer prosper. In his domain are proverbs, parables, innuendoes, incantations, libations, panegyrics, prophecies, rhapsodies, homilies and all the epithets of benevolence.

Due to his creative power/energy, the works of narrators, sculptors, painters, weavers, masons, minstrels, Ijala, Oriki and Ewi-poets cannot be completed without their turning to him for afflatus, guidance and flawlessness. Whosoever has *ase* in Yoruba land, has a formidable asset. Of all gods and goddesses, it is Divinity-Philosopher Orisanla who is given *ase* at the behest of Creator-Philosopher Olodumare. Bolaji Idowu (1962) put it thus:

He who makes eyes, makes nose;
It is Orisa I will serve
He who creates as he chooses
It is Orisa I will serve
He who sends me here
It is Orisa I will serve. (72)

Every creature serves Divinity-Philosopher Orisanla. D.O. Fagunwa had served him. Duro Ladipo had served him. Hubert Ogunde had served him. Amos Tutuola, Wole Soyinka, Niyi Osundare and other old and young men and women of letters are serving him. They must pay homage to him. They must serve him because without his blessing, their corpora will shrink into oblivion. One luminary (Bishop Ajayi Crowther, 1807–1891), preached against him after his conversion into a foreign religion and tongue. The preaching was so vigorous, so scathing and flaying that the British forgot to recognize some of the gods and goddesses on occupying the land in the middle of the nineteenth century. This, for example, is in contrast to Indian male and female deities which the British did not have the luxury to pooh-pooh. Today, nearly all the primordial Indian gods and goddesses have found favor and existence in the British dictionaries and encyclopedias, as do the Greek gods and goddesses. The Yoruba scholars and intellectuals are adjuring the compilers of these lexical books to the same to Yoruba gods and goddesses.

Long before any hominid put pen to paper, Divinity-Philosopher Orisanla had been improvising and had been in charge of creation of the earth and the arrangement of its trappings. Both the Object Writing and the writing as we know it today are attributed to Divinity-Philosopher Orisanla, as Egypt attributed hers to Thoth, god of all cultural elements as well as the goddess of Isis, as Babylonian mythology ascribed its to Nebo, god of destiny, as the ancient Chinese attributed theirs to a dragon-faced god, T'sangChieh, as the ancient Greece attributed hers to Hermes, as the Romans ascribed theirs to Mercury, as the ancient Mexico ascribed hers to Quetzalcoatl, and the ancient India attributed hers to Parajapati, who is linked closely with Brahman.

There are two stages of development of literature in Yoruba land. The first stage started from the time Divinity-Philosopher Orisanla landed on earth till circa 6. B.C when Jesus Christ was born. A period of theocracy, it was. The second stage was between 6 B.C. and the time a Portuguese sailor, arguably reached Yoruba land in 1485. The second stage was the peak of Ifa and ifamas (Ifa-mase), the festival of Orisas and kings; from which Christmas became a corruption. In other words, Christmas was derived from Ifamas. Ifa-Ife, an ineffable Bible of the land or the Book of Enlightenment is very indispensable. It has 256 books, known as Odu corpus, under the cultivation, prophecies and knowingness of Divinity-Philosopher Orunmila. (Orunmila was a corker, made to the character of a devout; happy in everything but putting no more faith in anything other than Ifa-Ife, the Book of Enlightenment or the Book of Knowledge, under his creditable and ingenious cultivation). Each Odu contains 800 stories which is 256 by 800, totaling 204, 800 stories. This book of 204, 800 stories contain theocratic ethics, epics, legends, adages, proverbs and theogonic myths as well as the public parables. Here is a typical Ifa poem as versed by the keepers of the traditions:

He was dancing
He was rejoicing.
He was praising his Ifa priests
He opened his mouth
And the song of Ifa entered therein
As he stretched his feet
Dancing caught them.

Ifa-Ife Divination, the autochthonous book of life, deals with all kinds of subjects. It is the Alpha and Omega of knowledge. And Divinity-Philosopher Orisanla is the loadstone, just as Solomon is the wiseacre of Christian Bible. Very often, we hear oracles saying that the first stage of literary development was the Old Testament while the second stage was the New Testament. Again, we hear the following from the keepers of traditions:

"He who ties cloth on the loins and moves gracefully
He who wears a garment and moves gracefully
The very hard stone
Ifa divination was performed for Good-home
Who was the wife of Orunmila
Good-home does not die
Good-home does not fall down
Good-home does not go to heaven
The door of Good-home is always opened by many
Ifa, her husband does not go to
heaven without coming back."

Whosoever creates the soul: creates Mother Earth. He once said to his children to go and multiply like the sand on the earth. To Divinity-Philosopher Orisanla belongs a Yoruba alphabet, the Yoruba realm of letters. Divinity-Philosopher Orisanla is not only a creator of all things on earth, he is also a linguist. In effect, all poets, all writers, belongs to him and he belongs to them. Your work cannot be propitious without believing in him. Can anyone be angry or ireful with the earth—Mother Nature without treading upon it?

Whosoever seeks the meaning of life, believes in Orisanla.
Whosoever believes in dreams, believes in Orisanla.
Whosoever believes in hereafter, believes in Orisanla.
Whosoever believes in lore and jinni, believes in Orisanla.

Whosoever believes in immortality of the world, believes in Orisanla.
Whosoever believes in festivals of imagination, believes in Orisanla.
Whosoever believes in hair-raising legends, believes in Orisanla.
Whosoever believes in good and evil, believes in Orisanla.
Whosoever believes in a Family Tree, believes in Orisanla.
Whosoever believes in oral literature, believes in Orisanla.
Whosoever believes in science fiction, believes in Orisanla.
Whosoever believes in science & technology, believes in Orisanla.

According to Tai Bola (personal communication, 1963), before Divinity-Philosopher Orisanla left his abode in heaven, Creator-Philosopher Olorun/Olodumare instructed him that if he believed in him, he would make him the father of all creatures that walketh and crawleth on the surface of the earth. The literary significance of Divinity-Philosopher Orisanla cannot be overstated; for whosoever knoweth, knoweth. Divinity-Philosopher Orisanla knows all the world languages. He is the protagonist and the rest of the world is his deuteragonists

Perhaps the writer who portrayed most the p's and q's of Divinity-Philosopher Orisanla in terms of words and deeds and chiaroscuro was D.O. Fagunwa (1950). In his oeuvre, Fagunwa was the deuteragonists while Divinity-Philosopher Orisanla is the protagonist. Probably that was why his books were said to be a link between heaven and earth. He was also said to be a personification of Divinity-Philosopher Orisanla's literary voice,for he was not only imbued with the genius of Creator-Philosopher God, he was also emblazoned with his worldviews. The following is a case in point:

Your Royal Highness, may Olorun bless you
with longevity. May Olodumare ward off
untimely death over you
May Orisanla stop any disease
from paralyzing you
May the Omnipotence save you from
near and far-away foes (35).

As part of his covenant with Divinity-Philosopher Orisanla, D.O. Fagunwa left the physical world for the abode of Creator-Philosopher Olorun in December 1963. He was at the acme of his literary profundity when he rose heavenwards. His disappearance was/is likened to the biblical takeoff of Elijah.

Epexegetically, it is widely believed that Divinity-Philosopher Orisanla knows the destiny as well as the name of every individual while still in the womb. He knows who is going to become an oracle teacher or preacher and who is going to become a tiller. He knows when abiku is going to be born and when a mother will give birth to Taiwo and Kehinde. Naming, unequivocally, is one of the cultural values in a Yoruba Family Tree. Putting it aesthetically and reminiscently, Derek Walcott (1930–2017) heard the keepers of traditions saying saying:

"A name means something
The qualities desired in a son,
and even a girl-child;
so even the shadows who called
you expected one virtue,
since every name is a blessing ."

Translation mine.

The second Divinity-Philosopher who has always been supportive of writers is Divinity-Philosopher Ogun, the commander of iron and steel. Like Divinity-Philosopher Orisanla, his first home is the holy city of Ile-Ife (Garden of Love, according to how this author refers to it literarily), cleared and guarded by him but created by Divinity-Philosopher Orisanla. He supports whatever man does, especially literary pursuits. Because he was industrious, he was asked by Divinity-Philosopher Orisanla to clear the gardens of the holy city Ile-Ife so that the Garden of Love was worth living and ideal for the children of the land to multiply. He is equally indispensable like Divinity-Philosopher Orisanla. He has to his credit as the only divinity who controls whatever man lays his hands upon to use. Without borrowing an opposition, Divinity-Philosopher Ogun is concerned with the physical part of a man, while Divinity-Philosopher Orisanla concerns himself with the intellectual part.

Practically everything one owns belongs to Divinity-Philosopher Ogun. An engineer, a tailor, a builder, a writer, a carver, a sculptor, even a cook, uses all the tools under the control and auspices of Divinity-Philosopher Ogun. When a writer enters his study, sits at his table, and starts to write, Divinity-Philosopher Ogun has already provided his physical part inasmuch as he will use a pen, a typewriter or a computer to write. But he cannot start writing until Divinity-Philosopher Ogun clears the way for him.

In his posh office, Dada Olujagun said, "I am a big boss already. I dictate to my secretary, so I don't make use of Ogun once I'm in my office." That was 1971 in Lagos. A few days later, the big boss said he heard a voice as he was sipping his cup of tea, saying, "even that cup of tea belongs to Ogun." Surely, it was not only the cup of tea but his entire Ogunate.

In broader terms, Divinity-Philosopher Ogun is not only the proprietor and overseer of all instruments. He is also an unconquerable warlord. Whether local or mother of all battles, they cannot start, nor can they end without Divinity-Philosopher Ogun being involved or consulted. He caused all the cultural wars in Yoruba land and it was him who ended them.

Divinity-Philosopher Ogun, like Divinity-Philosopher Orisanla is the Muse in the innermost recess of a poet. He is the pulse in the temple of a prose-writer. He claims to know the meaning and the use of each finger, adding that fingers clutch his implements every hour. Sometimes, Divinity-Philosopher Orisanla would impugn him for going too far, reminding him that he is his student and a student is not supposed to disdain his teacher. You don't have to apotheosize him before you know that he is part and parcel of your corporeal being. As a matter of fact, there is no hour or minute without being involved in what is divinity-philosopher Ogun and what divinity-philosopher Ogun is. Indubitably, Ogun is an everyday essence (consciously or unconsciously; his literary values are second to that of Orisanla, only, simply because Orisanla controls the intellect while he controls per se the vehicle of accomplishment. Dutifully, while Ogun proposes, Orisanla disposes, courtesy of ase. Man is a linchpin betwixt both of them.

Aware his research-student would write a book on Yoruba ritual performance, the director, versed in the chants and essence of Divinity-Philosophers Orisanla and Ogun, informed the researcher that they had only reached the end of chapter one. That was after the researcher had produced a work of almost 500 file-pages! Many rivers, yet the deep is not overflowing.

Apart from their dissimilar status quo, Divinity-Philosophers Ogun and Orisanla dwell in the same perspective confirming the saying that the voice of the Divinities is the voice of Creator-Philosopher Olodumare. Both of them believe that man rules the society while Creator-Philosopher Olorun rules the Divinities and the society. Hence it was impossible in those theocratic days to tell a mouthful of folklore without the *breath* of the kings and the gods. Even today, the obas or the kings still regard themselves as the rulers of the land even if the military (using Divinity-Philosopher Ogun's instruments), have virtually rendered them toothless. The sole desideratum is the royal scroll, said to have been hidden in the City-State of Ile-Ife, and which neither the king nor Divinity-Philosopher Orisanla and his prophet, Divinity-Philosopher Orunmila, seems to know its exact location. Professor Idowu feared that it must have been mistakenly "burnt" along with the alien books in 1485 (Idowu 1962, 207). Either case should not be a screen before the ubiquitous eyes of the prophet.

Though atrophy is overtaking the ancient divinities, creating some disturbing vacuum, we should not forget that Divinity-Philosophers Orisanla and Ogun are the duo we need to turn to, literally, just as non-believers turn to other muses.

Writing in the *Research in African Literatures, page 1, Volume 27, No. 1 of 1996,* Noureini Tidjani-Serpos blamed Divinity-Philosopher Sango for not waking up to the age of technology. The only deity in Yoruba pantheon to be blamed for lack of technology in the continent of blue blood and brown angels is Divinity-Philosopher Ogun and not Divinity-Philosopher Sango as explained below. Divinity-Philosopher Sango, the Divinity of thunder and lightning, has nothing to do with invention. Divinity-Philosopher Ogun, the Divinity of steel and iron, is the deity to be credited with any invention. Alongside his main métier, Divinity-Philosopher Sango is a defender of justice for one and all, and when he roars, with his eyes closed, the walls crumble, the trees shed their leaves, the sun and the moon cringe in an eclipse of shilly-shally. Moreover, he is an indefatigable theocrat, par excellence, from whom Duro Ladipo derived his vim as well as his fiery and inimitable ventriloquism and *sprechgesang.*

Blame it on Divinity-Philosopher Ogun. It was him who caused a division between Divinity-Philosopher Orisanla and himself. While Divinity-Philosopher Orisanla wanted the world to remain a pious citadel of cultural sublimity, Divinity-Philosopher Ogun desired to change the status quo--change the world from a cultural to a technological signature. The upshot was unethically fastidious. Because he fell out with Divinity-Philosopher Orisanla, he left Ile-ife (clad in a bloodstained uniform of rebuff, recalcitrance and brutality, looking every step like a warrior who would take no capitulation for a gory vanquishing) and pitched on a foreign soil, teaching the foreigners the use of iron and steel. First, the foreigners came to enslave his kith and kin. As though that was not enough, they came back again to occupy his beloved land and the struggle between culture on one hand, and science and technology on the other, continues. It continues since the industrial revolution started more than a century ago. Brother Noureini should remember that Divinity-Philosopher Ogun abdicated his rightful place for more than that. Remember too that the entire world is still swotting, reconstructing and transposing. None is perfect on either side of the coin.

However, had the two of them toiled and moiled together, Africa could have been the leader, and the hub of today's science and technology. This is no admission however, that Divinity-Philosopher Orisanla regrets the trappings of the earth, (God never regrets whatever he disposes), for he continues to argue that his cultural trappings and values are as indispensable as science and technology.

The scenario is a challenge; a challenge for all those involved in African literatures and their Diasporic imprints to labor together (researchwise) and convert Ifa from its present oral status to a written Holy Writ of monumental reference. Seeing that the chips are down, Professor Wande Abimbola has started to chart a course leading to a bodacious, commendable, fruitful and hermeneutic discourse.

Chapter Nine

Worshipping Creator-Philosopher Olodumare

VOICES FROM THE INNERMOST: voices from the dreams accrue to the instincts upon which the sacred realities are forged, letter perfectly and eudemonic ally. Those realities, they were, living, which philosophically confronted Divinity-Philosopher Oduduwa, as he occupied Ile-Ife (House of Love), building it as his sacred earthly city; tinged and cognate with an impeccable prosopographies.

In a foreign place, he found himself, thinking, musing over the days and nights that had brought him to a land in which he had to reign as the first citizen. Sometimes, he had questioned the rationale of his leaving heaven for an earthly abode where he had to acclimatize himself. Many times, had he felt lonely with little or nothing to do. After 256 days of philosophizing, the charismatic realized that Ile-Ife and her people would not succumb to a premature demise. "Ife will live as long as heaven lives," he said.

Consequently, he kowtowed and said, solemnly, "Obaluwaiye, when will your children see you face?" Creator-Philosopher Olodumare raised his hands and said, "You cannot see my face but you can feel my pulse by worshipping me. Your Creator knows about your concerns. Don't be afraid, I shall make your stay worthwhile."

That was a turning point in the history and culture of the Yoruba people; for a new word, *worship,* had been born in conjunction with Ifalogy, and the children now knew how to worship God by paying his divine honor which was either said or sung, the components of which are prayers, praises and sacrifices, holistically under a ritualistic and liturgical worship.

Divinity-Philosopher Oduduwa, the antecedent of the Yoruba, again heard Creator-Philosopher Olodumare say, "Your religion shall be called Ife," (Love). Some theorists believe that Ife (Love) is the same as Ifa; just as Ile-Ife is the same as Ife. The truth cannot be elusive beyond the next period since Ifa literally means "a pull." And love in its truest sense, "pulls" one or more people together. Pull is a noun as love is a noun. Thus, "Ife" and "Ifa" could arguably refer to one and only meaning. Thus the bible of the land has pulled its people together to love God in the niche of love.

On accepting Ifa-Ife Divination (the Book of Enlightenment or the Book of Knowledge) as the bible and the religion of the land, the people became more sure-footed in the society. Most mysteries were demystified. Shrines were built, and people could either worship privately or publicly, as the only means by which they could commune with their Creator. Fears were also dissipated. By worshipping Creator-Philosopher Olodumare, people could visualize where they were going and where they were coming from. Basically, what drew the believers by the droves is the Ifa Corpus and its universal message of peace and love.

Although Divinity-Philosopher Oduduwa opened the door leading to the cue of worshipping Creator-Philosopher Olodumare, the people did not worship him directly. As a matter of fact, they did not know how to worship him. They wondered worryingly whether they had to worship him by standing, kneeling or prostrating. When Divinity-Philosopher Oduduwa knew about their concerns, he said that everyone, young or old, male or female, should kneel down while worshipping Creator-Philosopher God, emphasizing the fact that the authentic beat-pulse of any religion is enshrined in its worshipping the Creator of heaven and earth. From that instance, they learnt how to pray; praise; sacrifice, and appease Creator-Philosopher God through his demythologized Divinities (orisas), amongst whom are the top-notch and the most prominent Divinity-Philosophers Orisanla or Obatala, Oduduwa, Orunmila, O'Sango, Ogun, Oya, Olokun, Oshun, O'Esu, O'Yemoja, Oshosi, O'Sopona, et al; for they thought if they could not see Creator-Philosopher God's face, they could at least behold the faces of his messengers. Most of the Tetragram's deities could be worshipped at anytime of the day. Some could be worshipped communally on a set day in a compound or in a shrine. Music, dancing, reciting, singing or chanting do accompany most communal worships, for Creator-Philosopher Olodumare listens to every rhythmic, melodious, harmonious and solemn sound created to honor him.

It must be asserted here that there is no undertaking that is not preceded by worshipping God, through prayers. It is your duty to worship Creator-Philosopher Olodumare whether you are a farmer, a tailor, a smith, a hunter, a singer, a drummer, a dancer or a carver. While men pray to have quality wives, women pray to have illustrious children. Wherever she prays, whenever she prays, the Yoruba woman, especially, had found that prayers are deeply tinged with eudemonism. In some cases, she finds herself more prayerful than her male counterpart.

Sacrifices, thank offerings, festivals, covenants, dedications, cleansing and forgiveness and the love for divine power and grace find their sense, belief, sanction and spirit in the worship of Creator-Philosopher Olodumare.

In the beginning, when the people were unsure-footed, some parts of the land had been reported to have sacrificed humans to worship God. But as the days went by, Divinity-Philosopher Oduduwa rejected the idea and then replaced dispensationally humans with the kola nuts and the four-legged animals such as the dogs. Since that day of a new wear of attitude, kola nuts have been the most propitious nuts of worship, while animals such as the dogs have remained the number one of all the sacrificial animals in the land. Immolation of birds such as roosters and pigeons are also common. Below is a tabulation of Ifalogy, the religion of the Yoruba in Africa and in Diaspora. It is the religion whose doctrines are akin to the doctrines of the Old Testament of the Christian Bible, printed in Germany in 1492. The home-grown religion sheds an iridescent light on Ifa-Ife, Ifalogy, the Book of Enlightenment or the Book of Knowledge as the Yoruba religion is variously described. Let's view the following tabulation:

Founded:	It was founded about the same time as the creation of the holy city of Ile-Ife.
Founder/Cultivator:	The founder/cultivator is Divinity-Philosopher Orunmila at the behest of Creator-Philosopher Olodumare.
Sacred Texts:	The 256 books of Odu Corpus which in turn contains 204,800 stories relating to the autochthonous worldviews of the Yoruba people, predicated upon religion, philosophical, sociology, history, anthropology and the literary corpora. It contains a vast number of epic and cosmological myths about

divinities—gods, goddesses and the antecedents. Ewi and Oriki are the most important of its poetry.

Practice: Originally theocratic, lfa has many priests and priestesses who conduct most rituals.

Division: The divisions are found in the various gods and goddesses worshipped, the most prominent of whom are Divinity-Philosopher Orisanla or Obatala, the Divinity of earthly creation; Sango, the Divinity of Thunder and Lightning; Ogun, the Divinity of sculpture, iron and steel.

Location: Mainly in Nigeria, the republic of Benin, Togo, North and South Americas and West Indies.

Beliefs: There is only one supreme God; Creator-Philosopher Olodumare, the Creator, the Author of Life and Death, under who are the messenger-gods and goddesses or the lesser deities who are answerable to him. Ase, the creative power every diviner seeks; for a diviner without ase is like a mouth without a tongue.

It is also believed that Christmas was derived from Ifamas, the festival of deities, priests and priestesses. It is the belief of the Yoruba people that Ile-Ife is the cradle of mankind.

Spiritual Gifts: Prophecies, divinations, incantations and mind-reading—by the prophets or diviners, otherwise known as priests and priestesses.

In Yoruba land, the shrine is the "countenance" of the divinity through whom Creator-Philosopher Olodumare is worshipped. And it is the priest or the priestess who leads and directs every communal service. She or he is the one who feels the pulse of the Creator and reveals the message to the worshippers. The deity or divinity is represented by the emblem which is regarded as adequate reminder of his attributes. According to Professor Bolaji Idowu, worshipping Creator-Philosopher Olodumare is worshipping "the President of the Domestic Life and Director of all Destinies."

It will be recalled that when the missionaries entered the Yoruba land in the nineteenth century and the jihad in the sixteenth century, they noted that the Yoruba had established their faith in the Almighty Creator-Philosopher Olodumare. Why did they then convert most Yoruba to Christianity and Islam, respectively? It was a long debate, we were told. When the Yoruba said they are strong believers in, and worshippers of Almighty God through his messengers, the converters riposted, "As long as you do not possess the Holy Books to show us, you may still want to follow the latest. Renounce Ifa and you will be showered with happiness, peace and abundance. In our religion, lies the salvation of the world!" Consequently, Ifa (sic) was relegated to the stygian corner of the shrine, while most of the land followed the wills and ways of the new religions and their convertors. Is that a sacred reality? Or shall we allow the posterity to ask whether it is a secular solecism? Are the Yoruba and the Ifa tinged with nostalgia?

Today, Creator-Philosopher Olodumare is worshipped prayerfully and reverently, both the missionary way and the Yoruba's way. God does not cry himself hoarse as long as he is divinely worshipped, either individually or congregationally; in an oratory or in a shrine of crosses and images. The next generation of believers will have to choose between the worshipping of Creator-Philosopher Olodumare and the worshipping of Yahweh, as well as Allah. But according to my interviewees (Christmas and Muslims alike), Ifa must be modernized like the royal houses, the social, economic and political institutions if it has to be on the same "footing salvation" with the Bible of the Christians or the Quran of the Muslims, which are the foreign embellishments, embellishing the Yoruba people with baits/crumbs (disturbing, cajoling, deceiving, manipulating, converting the innocent and regal people into a tantalizing paradise) like the baits/crumbs of the slavery or the slave masters.

Chapter Ten

The Yorubanized Messiah

"If the Yoruba philosophy, religion, history, sociology, anthropology and literature are combined to form a book, the book will be as universal as the Holy Writ" asserted Pastor Ademola, who according to him, has studied the Yoruba culture and the Bible from the Genesis to Revelation.

Inasmuch as Ile-Ife and Yoruba culture have been in existence before Christianity, it is not unlikely that the Creator must have visited Ile-Ife long before Jesus Christ was born in circa 6 B.C. The question most researchers usually ask is, "Is Oluorogbo the Messiah of Yoruba people?" If we can find prophets and prophetesses in Yoruba land as we can find them in Nazareth, then the similarity between the Christian Messiah and the Yorubanized Messiah will not be farfetched. If indeed Oluorogbo did come to save his people, therefore Christology and ifalogy will have the same "theocentric world" in common.

Let's go back in history about the printing of the Bible. The Bible was printed in Mainz, Germany in the mid-1450s. Johann Gutenberg and his boon companion, Johann Fust published more than 150 large format copies of the Bible in Latin, and the compilation was known as the Gutenberg Bible. Since then the Bible has shaped the religious history of the world just as the invention of the fairies in the 13th century by Gervase of Tilbury has shaped the history of the small beings.

The Gordian knot we are to untie is not the one betwixt the Christology and ifaolgy, nor will it be between Christendom and Ifadom. The knot to be untied is about the personality, called Oluorogbo. One version of the account before us is that Oluorogbo was born to Queen Moremi toward the end of the fourteenth century in Ile-Ife when the eternal city was engulfed by sheer lawlessness and disrespect for aesthetics. We are told (see chapter three) that Moremi helped to bring a speedy end to the strife between Ile-Ife and Igbo infantrymen by sacrificing Oluorogbo, her only issue, to a river goddess. Because Ile-Ife was delivered and the lawlessness was replaced with peace, students and researchers like Pastor Ademola believe that Oluorogbo is the Messiah who had come to the world to redeem the Yoruba from delinquencies, when the virtues and values were divorced from morality. That the Yoruba land was saved cannot be denied. That Moremi and Oluorogbo occupy an important chapter in the cultural history of the Yoruba people cannot be discountenanced. Nothing shall be disputed as long as the Elders and the keepers of traditions act like a chain, stretching from antiquity to the present.

The second version of the account is that Oluorogbo was an Abiku child who tormented his mother five times before he acquiesced to stay in the world of realities. Each one of her births was heralded by a warning to the king to redress the lawlessness in his kingdom. But the king refused to hearken to the voice of the diviners. However, Oluorogbo was born an Abiku child having tormented his mother five times. At last, he promised the diviners that he had come to stay. People were happy and his parents leapt for joy.

As months and years went by, the people could bear it no more. They started complaining. Libations to deities were infrequent and Creator-Philosopher Olodumare was no longer worshipped on a daily basis. Sooner than expected, the diviners came with the news that the young Oluorogbo had been selected by the deities to save his people. The stripling went from house to house reminding the occupants not to shirk their responsibilities to Olorun Oba. While some people yielded to his voice of salvation, others did not.

Consequently, the diviners delivered a new message; a message which surprised not only the subjects but also the king and his deputies. In the message, the diviners disclosed that the only way to put the kibosh on the lawlessness of the land was to sacrifice Oluorogbo to a river goddess. On hearing the divination, the charismatic cooed and cooing was like the music of the spheres.

After he had been sacrificed to the river goddess, peace and excellent government came back to Ile-Ife. Thus, the people identified themselves with another period of aesthetics.

To some, Oluorogbo was a victim of lawlessness and misguidedness. To others, he was a Savior of his people. Both versions of the story may fluctuate but what will decline to fluctuate like the virtues of Creator-Philosopher Olodumare is that one culture hero in the name of Oluorogbo was born in Ile-Ife to Moremi and her husband, Ajasoro.

Contemporarily, the intelligentsia and literati do not buy every account about the Yorubanized Messiah. We have heard different rhetoric. We have heard that Oluorogbo was carried away by two men on horsebacks on getting to the riverside where he was supposed to be given away to the goddess Esinmirin. Oluorogbo and the two horse riders went to the villages surrounding Ile-Ife, telling the villagers that they should return to the eternal city as the eternal city was at peace through the grace of Creator-Philosopher Olodumare.

Who the horse riders were, we have no information. We do not have information also as to what happened to the charismatic. However, the Elders believed that his mission was not limited to the eternal city and its environs alone. His mission was to deliver his message of peace to all the nooks and crannies of the Yoruba land. That only a few people heard about his mission outside Ile-Ife, is still a mystery. A mystery, it was also that no one could tell the identities of the men (possibly angels) on the horsebacks.

According to Pastor Ademola, Oluorogbo was indeed the Messiah who all the believers in Deism have been waiting for. He argued that the Divine Being will not send his angels (let alone his only begotten son) to any part of the world until he knows that part of the world is devoid of peace. Wherever there is decadence, there God will send his angel to redeem. Ile-Ife had its own Messiah, rather unsuspectingly. Other believers may have theirs with little or no inkling or admonition. Any Messiah is a harbinger of peace and a brand-new status quo. But when no one (Dei gratia) seems to hearken to his message of peace, he will disappear like Oluorogbo, murmuring thus:

I am an abiku
Abiku with an Amen of Salvation.
If the world does not love me
Heaven will love me.
Heaven is my abode
To heaven, I will go.

Fragmentary is the account (like all oral narratives) of Oluorogbo. Like Jesus Christ, his mission is a paradigm for the believers, for he had saved the souls of a people and had laid down his life without trepidation.

Chapter Eleven

The Covenants of the People

A COVENANT IS LIKE a deed or a contract performed inside a tabernacle, an oracle, or inside a cult fire. If you break it, it will burn you. (The chapter title of this page is inspired by The Covenant of the Earth which was published in 1998).

If you keep it, it will sustain your life into elderliness. There are many covenants in Yoruba land as there are words on a flippant tongue. But between God and man, there is only one covenant which is "betwixt heaven and earth." The earth has to obey the heaven in order to survive because the first religious covenant ever made was/is between the contiguous heaven and earth.

The Covenant is a prominent book in Ifa. The first letter between Creator-Philosopher Olodumare and Divinity-Philosopher Oduduwa was a covenanted deed in which God said, "The place where I am sending you to is a covenanted land. Do not treat it with sacrilege."Divinity-Philosopher Oduduwa obliged to do as God wished, promising the Infinite that his proxy would not shirk his responsibilities. Because Divinity-Philosopher Oduduwa walked with God, God made him the king of his people. It was not a king with an earthly crown but a king with a heavenly crown, otherwise known as halo.

Why did Ile-Ife become an eternal city? Ile-Ife became a prosperous city of eternity because Divinity-Philosopher Oduduwa, the theanthropic monarch did not break the covenant he made with God. Similarly, the people did not break their covenanted promises with Divinity-Philosopher Oduduwa. To all intents and purposes, the eternal city, otherwise called the land of covenants, became the pride of Creator-Philosopher Olodumare. Divinity-Philosopher Orisanla who had carried out his covenant without failing, was elated seeing that the holy city of Ile-Ife was booming with peace, love and dolce vita. So happy he was that he cried out in a spirit emblazoned with bliss, "Olorun Oba, if it is possible to stay with your anointed, I will, for I have done as ordered."

According to the Elders, the land of the covenants did not fall like a house of cards. Note well. Only its "covenanted values" started to disintegrate after Divinity-Philosopher Oduduwa had completed his mission and gone back to heaven. After his departure to heaven, the folk were unable to keep their covenants. It was at this juncture, the reigning Oba warned them that if they did not keep their covenants with Divinity-Philosopher Oduduwa, their kith and kin would sell them into slavery.

While still in the lap of luxury, something happened that stunned Ile-Ife and its extended families. What stunned the land is that Mr. Ijapa was found hiding behind the king's throne while the king-makers were preparing for the coronation of a king. Needless to say that he was charged with unlawful entry into the king's palace. For being the first to break one of the covenants of the people, he was whiplashed twenty-four times. Although his action was regarded a serious misdemeanor, a slap on the wrist, it was not rumored outside the palace. The outrage had been hushed up.

Since that time, mononymous Ijapa, the Babyface, had been instrumental to both light and serious misdemeanors. Because he involved himself in everything that occurred in the land of covenants, with respect to folklore, he gave himself funny names such as bête noire, recidivist, recalcitrant, mind-set, and a conception of successes and failures as well as a sponger in the house of hospitality. On realizing that he was now the warp and weft of the culture, the folk entitled him a "folk-honey." Thus he became an indispensable protagonist in every folktale of value and substance. As a matter of research, no folktale shall ever claim a measure of hair-raising and completion without a role played by the folk-honey.

About the age of 25, mononymous Ijapa became a popular tailor in the holy city of Ile-Ife. He could sew any kind of men's and women's attire. He was so popular that bachelors and spinsters made his shop the cynosure of tete-a-tete and table talk. His only ambition in life was to buy the best mask in the land and a plot of land upon which to build his own house. Buying the best mask and having his personal house was the yardstick with which he had measured any kind of success.

When success did not smile on his face, he collected his belongings and left the eternal city as early as the first glimpse of the sun, for Oyo. In Oyo he became a barber after six months of intensive training.

At about the age of 29, he was the most popular barber in town. Again his barber shop, on the crest of a hill, was the cynosure of tete-a-tete and table talk among artists, young and old. He was versed in all kinds of hairstyles except those beyond the compass of human mind. However, his dream remained the same; that is to buy a first-class mask and to purchase a land upon which to build his own house.

At about the age of 33, he was shilly-shallied and confused by the vicissitudes of life. One harmattan day, he dressed up foppishly and left for Ogbomosho in search of yet another dream of success. Here he became a builder after nine months of intensive drilling. Mr. Ijapa could fabricate anything from the garden furniture to fishing canoes and boats. He had the knack of building roads too. He had a phenomenal dexterity. Having said that, he was again the talk of the town. A fop and the most eligible bachelor in the land has been born, the townees would whisper. The news flared across the land of the covenants like a red tongue of flame leaping out of the sky during the harmattan season. The wild fire became a metaphor of destruction, only to be tempered by showers of love. Out of that metaphor arose questions such as "Is he impotent? Is he going to pass away without an issue? Hasn't he someone to advise him?

One late evening, on his way home, having dined with a friend, he saw a minstrel and a mendicant, separated by a stretch of about twenty yards from each other. Soon, he heard them singing thus:

Baby-face, Baby-face, face the truth
Winnow truth from falsehood
Life is a mystery
Your success may depend on a
Partner's religious love
Baby-face, Baby-face, face the truth.

He paid little or no attention to the song, not when he had just relished a sumptuous dinner.

Discomfited by the news and the song, his parents sent him an urgent message. In the message, they disclosed how worried they were seeing a bachelor at the age of 34. He riposted by saying "success begets everything in life."

Said his parents, "You know your brothers and sisters have all married?"

Baby-face, knitting his brows said, "Yes, I know."

His parents again asked, "Are you a fortune hunter?"

"No."

"There are four stages in life: the crescent, the half moon, the gibbous and the full moon. You're now a full moon and a full moon must have a love of his own. Are you a full moon?"

"Yes I am," answered Mr. Ijapa, the Baby-face with a perceptible nod and a winsome smile.

Baby-face was faced with paradoxical sleeps and scary nights. The reason is that he started pondering over what his parents had told him: "You are a full moon and a full moon must have a love of his own."

On his 35th birthday anniversary, Baby-face packed his bag and baggage and returned to the land of the covenants. At the end of that year, he erected once again his barber's pole and enjoyed his trade as a barber of style and sartorial popularity.

A year later, the first quarter of the year, when the flowers were blossoming, and the doves were cooing the arrival of the rainy season, mononymous Ijapa, the Baby-face fell in love with a woman of his dreams. Before that year ran out, he was able to purchase a first-class mask, as well as a plot of land upon which he built his dream house. Success, he agreed, had now started to smile on his face. He was happy to learn that a covenant is a conditional promise made between humanity and Creator-Philosopher Olodumare as contained in the oracle and rituals of Ifalogy.

The Yoruba land today, still regards a covenant as a bond between heaven and earth. But unlike the heyday, covenant-betrayers are rarely flayed. Every Yoruba man or woman knows what a covenant stands for, as he or she knows the value of a prayer. Because a covenant is a contract, first between God and his anointed, and then between the anointed and his people; that is why parents of a baby of eight days have to, willy-nilly, initiate the baby into a covenant of longevity. By allowing the baby's feet to touch the earth, by allowing the baby to taste the eatables and drinkables, the baby has joined the "earthly-world" of living where covenant-making is both human and divine.

COVENANT-BASED SYLLOGISM

A covenant is a conditional life-promise made to } **} major term** humanity by Olodumare as destined by Ifalogy. }

Breaking a covenant	=	Death
Death	>	Betrayer
Betrayer	<	Death.

Keeping a covenant Life **} middle term**

* Keeper of a covenant= Life = Continuity }

Therefore, breaking a Covenant is human.
Keeping it (unbroken) is divine.

To be human = (earthly)= mortality.

} minor premise

To be divine = (heavenly) =immortality }

* Keeper of a covenant = Life = Continuity

PART THREE

LITERATURE

Author's Lodestar and Abridged Memoir of Mentalism, Religion and Literature

(The Calm Strength of Literary Philosophy)

If I should occupy myself by remembering the land of great antiquities, if I should recount all the artistic and the literary pleasures derived from my years of innocence, cognate with tableaux, if I should reflect upon the pleasures of memory and imagination from the years of childhood, I would feel full of vim due to my adrenaline glands. Grateful I am. I will feel sublime from inside to the outside and from outside to the inside, as though the descendants of the slavers had settled the reparations for purloining our ancestors from the continent of blue blood. My appetite for literature (my propaedeutic genre) will continue to increase, as I grow from year to year, while my appetite for comestible will be controlled or circumscribed by the pleasures obtained from the reams of writings. For good literature, which is the foundation of pleasures (like music rather than the media) nourishes the human emotions, reaffirms the present and reconstructs the future. These ethical and rational beliefs and assertions are inexhaustibly fundamental and interesting by the contents of their canons of conduct.

Relating all this with mankind and seeking the pleasures of relationships are the greatest sources of happiness that one can derive from the calm strength of humanity, regaling upon the virtue of philosophy, literature and arts, yes—true to the province of aesthetics.

The calm strength of love, found in humanity and the feeling of writing, dovetailing with the artistic virtuosity is like the feeling derived from listening to the delicious music of the spheres. An intellectual had asked, "Why do you write?" I write because my writing could become one of the soft-pedaling means to promote/enhance peace and love around the world. I write because the mortals and immortals expect me to write. I write because I want to be read, and read others. I write because I have fallen head over heels in love with letters, books and the power of words. I write because Creator-Philosopher Olodumare is my teacher and my director and my giver who always gives me mints of ideas that filter through my mind. I write because I invariably find an organic happiness in writing. I write because writing qualifies me to belong to the class/league of sciences and the humanities. I write because writing therapeutically distils my mind. I write because I want my writing to belong to the archives and libraries of immortality. I write because writing helps me link my existence to saints, angels, geniuses and heroes. I write because I want the Oversoul to explain to me why there are so many mysteries and tragicomedies in the world. I write because I want my writing to refresh the memories of the loved ones whose departures make my heart trapped in melancholy. I write in order to know myself and what myself can do to help everyone, my neighbor, since everyone is my friend with the charity of love. I write because I want my writing to inform, enlighten, entertain, educate, inspire, charm/enchant, and above all, inoculate the world with the ingredients of wellness, corporeal and spiritual happiness, likened to the thrills of a sweet dream with a beddable inamorata.

On noticing that I am still one-third a writer I would love to be, my parents who always stand on ceremony, in their hours of happiness, nobility, pleasantries and gleam of humor, demand of me the loftiest, the best, the crème de la crème, the noblest and the most supreme that I can do, but much that I could by no possibility have done, in order to belong to the league/class of sciences and the humanities, and be guided by the literary philosophy, and the power of words, as reason guides the human soul to nirvana or sasarawa.

Chapter Twelve

The Divine Voice of Kings

FROM TIME IMMEMORIAL, VOICE has been described asa spirit perched on the gossamer of life. Every creature therefore has that spirit which perches on the thread of life. A voice is also seen as a breath of life. The voice of Creator-Philosopher Olorun to his kings on earth is not any less important than the voice of the king to his subjects. For this reason, we often hear the saying, "The voice of Creator-Philosopher Olodumare is the voice of man."

When Divinity-Philosophers Orisanla, O'Sango, Orunmila, Ogun, Ayelala and other divinities first landed on earth, the only covenant between them and Creator-Philosopher Olodumare was the voice, a divinatory voice, under the domain of Divinity-Philosopher Orunmila. In those days of oral literature, a voice was like an unwritten constitution. Obeying the voice of Divinity-Philosopher Orisanla, Ayelala went round the earth. On coming back, he confirmed that the earth was big in consequence of his earthly name, Ayelala. His heavenly name was Orunlala, meaning the heaven is big. Soon after Ayelala's round the world trip, Divinity-Philosopher Orisanla confirmed to all the gods and goddesses that the earth was big enough for all their voices, and the holy gourd.

Based on what we were told regarding hagiology, the only voice in force during theocracy was the voice of Creator-Philosopher Olodumare, as well as the voices of Divinity-Philosophers Orisanla and Orunmila, the only divinities who were credited with the divine voice of Omnipotence.

After the completion of the creation of the earth, God asked all the theocrats to leave for the heavenly abode. They were no longer to stay on earth but in heaven. Moons later, he sent Divinity-Philosopher Oduduwa to rule Ile-Ife. Divinity-Philosopher Oduduwa who had both divine and human characteristics was not only grateful to Creator-Philosopher God and consanguineous divinities, he also (as we shall see later), gave the ancestors/pedigrees a sumptuous send-off party.

Having assumed his royal status through the voice of Creator-Philosopher Olorun, Divinity-Philosopher Oduduwa received the staff of creation. Thereafter, he heard the voice of God telling him to rule his subjects by divine voice and right of kings, while enjoying the immemorial privileges of the theocrats. The period of spiritual hierarchy was said to be between the creation of the earth and the birth of Jesus Christ in 6 B.C.

The oral historians noted that Divinity-Philosopher Oduduwa prospered because Ife turned out to be a propitious land. We were told he married and had nine male children who at the behest of their father's voice left the City-State of Ife and founded nine towns which they reigned over as Obas/kings, making use of the divine right of kings. This was the period Ife assumed its compound name, Ile-Ife: meaning the house has expanded. Those nine towns were the original towns in Yoruba land whose kings de jure, carry scepters and wear golden crowns of oracular authority.

The first case Divinity-Philosopher Oduduwa would preside over was a case of a family whose two young children were albinos. First Divinity-Philosopher Oduduwa did not want to pay much attention to the plaint brought against Divinity-Philosopher Orisanla, a comrade of his. But sooner than expected, Divinity-Philosopher Oduduwa heard Creator-Philosopher Olorun's voice saying Divinity-Philosopher Oduduwa should preside over the case so that he, Creator-Philosopher Oduduwa or Olorun could envision how he would rule as a theanthropic monarch.

Soon a date was set for the preliminary hearing. All the equerries and ministrants of the land were present. None but all were curious to hear the reason why a citizen of the land was accusing an arch-divinity. Like many accounts from the lips of historians, that was probably an omen that the kingdom, on reaching its zenith of prosperity would decline, at least, if falling could be prevented.

"I have no problem with Orisanla, until I have my first and second issues, all albinos" said lya-Afin, the plaintiff.

"You mean Orisanla was to blame?" asked a ministrant. "Absolutely so: he cannot exonerate himself."

"How come you are not contented for having two bouncing kids?"

"Will you be contented for giving births to albinos? Orisanla is the maker of the physical part of human beings. As a young mother, I desire all children but albinos."

"If he has no power to cure your children, why did he then create them?"

"Are you asking me that? Are you a foreigner to know the prerogative of an earthly creator in a regenerate society?"

The silence fell upon the meeting like the silence of the night. A city-state has been born; born to a people to live in, learn and feel the poetry of nature. It is a state where anything hardly goes wrong, as long as one listens to the divine voice. It is a state where one is supposed to enjoy the wisdom, the protection and the public spirit of the Kings and their Queens. A nation of one people, one mythical voice, one folkloric voice, one Family Tree, one cultural beau monde and one Olodumare, should not perish but survive. These lines of thought beat across the plaintiff's innermost. It was crystal-clear to her that it would take some time before she could start to understand the do's and don'ts of a creator in the theocratic government of Divinity-Philosopher Orisanla.

"What are you going to do now?" asked an equerry, squinting and knitting his brows.

"I'm going to implore Oba Oduduwa to take over the case."

"Why don't you forget about the case and ask Orisanla to provide you with as many children as your house could contain?"

"I don't need a houseful of albinos. A house built in your country is worth more than ten in a foreign land. You know what I mean?"

"Yes I do. May I suggest that you forgive and forget all?"

"To forget that it is my right to have good-looking children? Impossible. It is impossible. Of course, that's what most mothers say. They say I should not report him, that I should wait for Olorun to voice his ultimate opinion." She emphasized the last two words with a wry and a nod of her head.

"I hope it is lighter to be warned by Oduduwa rather than face the dressing-down of Creator-Philosopher Olorun or Olorun. God's dressing-down is too thrashing to bear. It is wise to have the matter settled by the king, my opinion and the opinion of my husband."

After one hour of listening to lya-Afin, the equerries and the ministrants brought the meeting to a close. The next meeting, an open-air meeting would be held at the beginning of a royal festival. It sounded as though it was adjourned sine die because there were many royal festivals. This time the king would be present. He was the only one whose royal voice lya-Afin wanted to hear. An anthropomorphic voice of his person could not be wrong.

The first royal festival came and passed, there were no words about a meeting. The third festival was about to take off when the town crier went round the town summoning one and all to an open-air court meeting between "heaven and earth."

It was a sunny Friday afternoon. Theocratic and human heads were basking under the tropically bluish sky. The meeting was big and semicircular. About three hundred people were in attendance, young and old. The medley of colored dresses was spectacular. Unlike the previous meetings held inside the royal compounds, this one was pitched along the bank of a man-made lake, called lake Divinity-Philosopher Orisanla. The seating was arranged as if there was a boating race, a fishing festival or a swimming competition. All the people except the equerries and the ministrants were facing the body of water.

Apart from king/Divinity-Philosopher Oduduwa, the next persons in prominence were Chiefs Ede, Eke and Ata. Iya-Afin was particularly amazed by the palindromes of the names of the Chiefs. She sat down in the middle, still nursing the ire of the first meeting, and wondering why it had taken so long for the second meeting to be convened.

An equerry whose face was laced with facts and figures, called the meeting to order, and Chief Ede stood up to speak: "Whenever there is a misunderstanding between heaven and earth, we call upon Creator-Philosopher Olodumare to voice his opinion. Whenever there is a quarrel, we settle it by the help of the Obas. If there is no Oba, we approach the Chiefs, and if there is no Chief, we call upon the Elders. This is our custom before the theocratic government was replaced by the divine voice of the kings. It is my hope this tradition will continue to be passed from one generation to the other."

A brief period of silence gave the king and the Chiefs a moment of putting their heads together after which Chief Ata stood up and asked the plaintiff to present her case. As the plaintiff stood up to present her case, Oba Oduduwa said, "Stop. Stop. Stop. Procrastination is the thief of time. Already, I know the nitty-gritty of the matter concerning your displeasure with your albino children. You have spoken. A good woman must continue to speak about matters regarding her children. Let Baba-Afin also stand on his feet.

"I have two questions for both of you after the following anecdote. This anecdote is important because it helped to identify the first lawyer of this land. For those who do not know that, this is the anecdote to back it up. There was once a rich man, a farmer, who lived in Ajao. He had neither wives nor children. But he was wealthy, blessed with yams. His compound was like a market of yams. One day, while on his farm, a billy-goat broke into his fenced compound and ate quite a number of his yams. On reaching home, he met the animal bleating gleefully. He slipped a rope around his neck and tied him to a post inside his kampong.

"The following day, the owner of the Billy-goat, a woman, came questioning the man for tying her belonging. The rich man said that the Billy-goat had not only broken into his compound but that he had also devoured more than two dozen of his yams. The woman was impatient to listen. All that she wanted back was her goat. A confrontation ensued. Eventually, the case was brought before the Elders and the Elders resolved that inasmuch as the Billy-goat had eaten the yams, the rich farmer had the right to keep him as his property. Thus the confrontation came to a peaceful end, and the Elders who settled the case became the primary lawyers and judges in all matters or disputes involving one or more parties.

"First question: What will you do if you were to be the owner of the Billy-goat?"

"I will not contest the farmer's decision to own the goat," said lya-Afin and Baba-Afin simultaneously.

"How many children are you asking Orisanla to bless you with?"

"Eight."

"You have answered correctly both questions, especially the first one. The rich man kept the goat in order to make the woman realize that it was important to watch over her pet. She got back her pet after three markets. I must emphasize that that was neither tit for tat nor pepper for honey, because it was unethical to ask the sin of an animal on its owner. That is not going to happen as long as the voice of Creator-Philosopher Olodumare is the voice of his people. Again, this numinous ground does not encourage retaliation.

"Now then, as the rich man had the right to keep the goat, as temporary as it was, so also Orisanla now has the right to keep his albinos. In addition to this, Orisanla will increase the number of your children from eight to nine; five boys and four girls. Are you satisfied?"

All of a sudden, husband and wife leaped up for joy and shouted, "satisfied" at the top of their voices. Consequently, all the people in the meeting stood up and applauded king Divinity-Philosopher Oduduwa for his exceptional wit. Thus, the Oba was proclaimed the wisest personage in Yoruba land, conflating the old with the new voice. He assumed the title "Oni," an ellipsis of Oni-Ile (Lord of the earth), a title bestowed upon him moons after he was proclaimed the wisest judge cum king in the land. Creator-Philosopher Olodumare did not renege on his promise. His voice came to Divinity-Philosopher Oduduwa, making him a powerful leader, a ruler of strong repute, selflessness, an embodiment of a thousand seminal ideas and an oracular authority of all that is in the holy city of Ile-Ife.

A few days later, Divinity-Philosopher Oduduwa gave his consanguineous friends and their female counterparts a sumptuous send-off party that lasted from sun up till sun down. But the deities, we were told, had multiple entry visas between heaven and earth, for they used to visit Ile-Ife from time to time.

One thing though, still remains a closed book with respect to the history of Divinity-Philosopher Oduduwa. No one knows how and when he paid his debt to nature. There are two schools of thought: one propounded that he died in Ile-Ife. Another version speculated that because he was imbued with Creator-Philosopher Olodumare's characteristics, it was not unlikely that he withdrew to heaven at the behest of Creator-Philosopher Olorun's voice. Both versions are plausible since there is no written record to support them.

His monumental heirloom, now a legacy, is the fact that he bequeathed to the Yoruba royal houses or families both the divine voice and the divine right of kings.

Voice is a spirit perched on the thread of life. Wherever there is a voice, there will be a sound. Wherever there is a sound, there will be words or letters. Wherever there are snippets, there will be life. Life came to the holy city of Ile-Ife the very moment there was a voice, a divine voice, divining the creation of the earth.

Chapter Thirteen

What is Creative Writing?

WHAT IS *CREATIVE WRITING*? Prior to the answer, let us say with a stress and rhythm that everyone can write and people write all over the world, every hour, everyday; putting down on paper words from the pages of their lips, on emanating from the faculty, the head, the powerhouse and the definition of the body, the substrate unto which other parts of the body are answerable.

The following are the ten principal ways to power your creative fiction/ story to success. These ten principal ways, we will call the *story openers*, as contained in Studying Creative Writing in Nigeria, published in 1991. They are:

1: Create complex characters, for characters are the personalities that populate your story. Your story is passionate to tell how your characters look like, and how they think, act and feel.

2: Selecting the Setting: This is about the where and when of your story.

3: Plan of Your Plot: Plan your story so that your story is imbued with creative or a literary sense.

4: Applying a Point of View: Apply a point of view that tells your story from a particular outlook.

5: Count Down to the Climax: This is where people expect the exciting moment they have been waiting for.

6: The First Sentence: Remember that your first sentence should be able to stir and het your reader's appetite.

7: Foreshadowing: What do we mean by this? We mean the herald of a sign or something to come. Therefore, use foreshadows to give your readers the clues about what is ahead.

8: Metaphors: Metaphors are the cookies that tantalize your readers' figments of imaginations. Good and poignant metaphors vividly paint your story or give the contents of your story an opalescent picture of what you are narrating. In other words, metaphors make your stories picturesque, much as they make them charming and entertaining.

9: Similes: Similes are the spices that add rich flavors to your story. They employ such words as *like*, or *as*.

10: Synonyms: Use as many synonyms as your afflatus tells you, for synonyms are the sentences that help your readers relish (with gusto) words with the same meanings as another in the same language but often with different implications and associations.

Now then, back to the question. What is Creative Writing? Creative Writing (like a brainchild), is the writing that comes from new ideas, born out of figments of imaginations. These are the ideas that pour forth from your soul, from your mind, from your heart, all of which originate from the head (ori), the definition of the body and the substrate to which all the parts of the body are answerable, as stated earlier, above. Creative Writing is similar to Creative Thinking which is the combination of research ideas and literary experiences, and transforming those ideas into new ways of reasoning, thinking and writing.

Before a person can become a writer, a serious writer for that matter, he or she must be baptized or initiated spiritually with some basic experiences. He or she must learn how to fall in love with dreams, with people, with environment, with days and nights. Quintessentially, these are buttressed by history, sociology and philosophy. Accomplishing these is to relish the aesthetics of writing and natural virtues.

There are three conditions from which you can derive figments of imaginations. First, you must derive your writing experience as you go from one place to another. Second, you derive your experience from what you touch and feel. Third, you derive your experience from what you see, touch, feel, hear, read as conditioned by Divinity-Philosophers Orisanla and Ogun. All these accrue to your market-place of ideas, for even the slightest thing you did at the age of four could rudimentarily be important.

Creative Writing which is principally a combination of prose and verse starts from the day you stepped into this world which is otherwise known as a temporary market of sell or buy. Creative Writing may be a natural marriage of prose and verse, we cannot gainsay the fact that poetry is the genesis that first opened the initial chapter of the world of words and the world has uncountable chapters. In other words, the whole word is poetry, meaning the creation of the world.

All the writings in our holy books are prophetic poetry. Everything you're; everything you do is poetry. The Oni palace, from its foundation to its cupola is poetry. The first smile: the first mimicry, the first cry "mo wa, mo wa, mo wa," on the lips of a newborn is poetry.

Every thought of yours is poetry. Unequivocally, each one of the 26 alphabets is poetry; for every thought, every dream is a page, every page, a tongue of words.

Poetry is a river of metaphors, coming from a spiritual rise, and flowing into a soft loamy or hydrous plane, forming divergent outlets, a delta information; the upshot of which is a prose, a lore, (fairy-lore, bird-lore, fish-lore, animal-lore, human-lore, etc).

As pointed out earlier, poetry is everything, anything you can possibly think about /of. It is within every step you take. Imagine walking from one end of a soccer field to another; the number of steps you take, is the number of poems you can couch. In a shorter version, poetry is a sacrifice offered to elicit the wheels of thoughts.

Imagine yourself in a virgin wood, watching the serene firmament, listening to the voice of nature which is poetry, as you find yourself surrounded by the flimsiest creations such as cobwebs and gossamers.

Poetry is an extension of a prose story, any story. Imagine yourself in a boat, paddling from Island A to Island B. by the time you get to Island B, you discover that you've already improvised something and that something is a story. The similar experience you had during which time you wrote a three-page narrative while travelling by bus from the holy city of Ile-Ife to the imperial city of Oyo, for an example.

Words are always there for the mind that wills. Words are the primary tools for a serious mind, for I simply refuse to admit that there are born-writers. No one is a born writer. However, one can become an initiated writer.

Having been initiated, you will have to feel from time to time that your fingers help to determine your emotional and innermost personality as you grow from day to day, becoming a writer.

ON WRITING THE WORD,
Write and what each letter in *write* means.

W -------------------------- Way

R --------------------------Right

I -------------------------- Inside

T --------------------------Teach

E------------------------ Explain

Every writer has demonstrated unconsciously the mystery surrounding the power and the use of fingers.

In sum and substance, being a creative writer, one has the following to remember, always:

NEVER A DAY WITHOUT A LINE
BE BOLD
BE CURIOUS
BE PAINSTAKING
BE CONFIDENT
ALWAYS FALL IN LOVE WITH LETTERS, BOOKS AND THE POWER OF WORDS.

The Advantages of Creativity: Since everyone can write, (so we believe in our literate societies such as America, France, Britain, Russia, Germany, Japan and Canada), we want to talk about creativity. Creativity is the act of creating; the noun form of being creative. Hence to be creative is to be imaginative and inventive. Creativity is therefore the spring-board whose impetus leads to Creative Writing and other forms of creativities, associated with the minds and the hands.

The more you create, the better you can control your emotions, and the longer and fresher your memory will be. In short, those who are adept at creating things in whatever forms and shapes, do not easily lose their memories in their old age. This theory has been proved to be true between 1983 and 1994, a period of my intense Creative Writing and research in

African Literatures. Between this period, I had the opportunity to interview six people.

In 1983, I met a ninety year old pensioner in Austria. He was a carpenter before he retired. His eighty-five years old wife was a full house-wife during her active years. While the husband could remember vividly the ins and outs of his trade twenty years back, his wife could hardly put together a clear picture. The older octogenarian would jocularly say that his spouse could not remember her past due to the love of her utensils. She was at sea.

The second interview was conducted in Nigeria in 1989. It was between two male octogenarians. One was a fisherman. The other was a palm-wine tapster. The fisherman could recall not only how he used to mend his fishing nets but was also able to recall the names of each fresh-water fish of every description. The tapster was asked about his occupation; all he could remember amounted to, "Those were my palmy days." No doubt, he was at his wit's end.

The third groups of people, also in their eighties, were interviewed in India in 1994. I have chosen octogenarians because at eighties, one is considered, gerontologically to have reached two thirds of one's life-span. They were a couple. The woman was eighty-one and the man was eighty-nine. Both of them were traders who lived by selling stationery during their salad days. But the woman veered to combine selling with sewing. Whenever the stationer closed her store, her last chore of the day was to sew old and new garments. Luckily enough, the interview was held in the presence of their first-born who burst out laughing whenever his father wryly denied seeing his better-half sewing at home. The male-stationer ended his recounting by saying that his wife did all her sewing in the store. All he could recall was that both of them were invariably busy, making money by selling the stationery. Their son was a witness and a bridge to their young days which his mother did not forget.

The advantages of creativity are many and varied, yet you have to be creative continuously before your entire constitution is spiritually involved: before creativity becomes the warp and weft of your inner-most being. For, as the mind proposes, the hand disposes. And there is always a "creative communication" between the mind and the hand. The mind is like a talking drum, while the sound is the product of its beat-to-talk. If you don't beat the drum, nothing shall be created, nothing shall be heard, and the mind shall be closed like a coconut without an opening. This is yet another reason why those who "keep themselves creative" have the ability to recount things at dotage without a loss of memory which is otherwise called Alzheimer's disease.

By doing something: by creating anything whatsoever by hand, or by writing, you shy away sixes and sevens, worries, sorrows and paroxysms of boredom, depression or impatience are forever defied and defeated without panic-stricken confusion.

Powerful minds: an uncompromising mind is needed while journeying to the bent of one's ambition in life. They had lived. They are living today. Genius minds of those who could mirror the past and presage the future. Surely, the mind is the seat of all inventions and figments of imaginations: inventions and imaginations which are constantly changing, as a result of the minds and the hands, working together as a team. There are many occupations in this day and age that keep minds as well as the hands busy, and Creative Writing is simply an integral part of a whole gamut of today's professional occupations, small or big.

According to Divinity-Philosopher Orisanla's reams of writings, as well as mints of capital ideas, whosoever creates words, creates a world that grows old only, but never dies. However, before the present system of education was introduced into the Yorubaland, the present Yoruba people neither read nor wrote in the Western sense of the terms. They communicated with one another by a system of material symbols, otherwise known as the Object Writing.

MULTI-PURPOSE RESUME

Use the sun to your advantage
Use the moon to your advantage
Use the stars to your advantage
Breath of my creation.
Go to the world: multiply the breath
I've given to you.
Create as you wish, as reason guides
The human soul
Follow your mind as you desire
Not for your multi-purpose
Holy gourd; this breath
this cure-all,
Is but for the four corners of the world

Uncountable creations
Like the stars on the navel of the sky
Uncountable creations
Like the sand on the palms
of the earth.
A Daily coign of vantage
Create, now, in our element, for the sands
are running out.

An imaginative literature which is a fountain-head of pleasure (like music) rather than information, nourishes human emotions, re-affirms the present and reconstructs the future, cognate with the facts and figures, asserting and confirming that learning is a cumulative process.

Chapter Fourteen

The Crisis of a Would-Be Title-Holder

MYTHS IN YORUBA LAND are as common as daisies on a watered field. They are as tagmemic as Yoruba vowel harmonies. They are as polysemic as the proverbs in the holy city of Ile-Ife. A myth occurs wherever a religion exists. As there is no culture without a religion, so also there is no settlement without a crisis-myth. In short, myths are stories that play hide-and-seek between known and unknown. Additionally, a myth is an expression of truth of existence in a form of a story. A myth can also be described as an imagination of a story. It is inexhaustibly interesting to uncover that the histories of the myths or mythologies are the histories of the world, worldly.

In the past, holding titles was competitive. Having and not having a title could ignite a jealous conflict of fatality. A titleholder is highly regarded even today. Holding a title is an authority by itself. It can make man both honorable and authoritarian. It can as well make him a polygamist. He can even become a polyglot or polymath by learning the tongues of his many wives and concubines. A titleholder or a coroneted king or queen is the mouthpiece of his or her subjects. It is an undisputed kolanut of camaraderie that a community without a crowned head is like a mouth without a tongue.

This historical narrative you are about to hear occurred during the last quarter of the nineteenth century. The Yoruba land had again begun to enjoy another acme of stability, prosperity and plenitude of Mother Nature. The obaship was reconstructed, giving the colonial masters the joy and excitement of sending their District Officers to the major royal divisions of the land.

The red-hot eye of the sun was emerging from the sky, behind the red mangroves. It would take probably another one hour before its effects could be felt by the Oyako villagers because it was during the harmattan. This was the time of the year when Oyako villagers had to wait for hours before they started to enjoy its radiant and therapeutic energy.

Gedu, just pushing forty, left Oyako village as early as the second cockcrow. Accompanying him were his only son, Raradi, twenty; and his domestic servant, Akoko, twenty-one. He came to his hunting but in a glade encompassing an old abandoned kolanut farm. Here, the three of them breakfasted. Having changed into his hunting suit, he asked his son to follow him, leaving behind his domestic servant to face the shadowy solitude of a hunting hut.

Perched atop an araba tree, with his son; a gun in hand, he was awaiting the arrival of the hyena. About twelve yards away was a kitten which he had tied up as a bait for the hyena. Akoko was still alone in the hunting hut, about 1000 yards away from the araba tree.

Gedu knew it was only during the harmattan, and during the early hours of the day that the hyena could easily be shot as he would emerge from the bushes of afrormosia, searching for his breakfast.

Suddenly, the sun which had been struggling to pierce through the firmament disappeared under a rain-bearing cloud. In another minute, it started to rain heavily. Father and son were feeling cold. Their clothes were sodden with rain. The doves had started cooing. The monkeys, jumped and clambered from trees to trees, chattering. The singing of the nightingales was the only sound that kept up his spirits, as well as the spirits of his son.

They waited and waited under such a poor weather condition, and now they began to feel that waiting there in order to kill a wild animal was less important than their health, now threatened by a chilling cold.

Suddenly the hyena leapt out of the bushes and other animals kept their silence. They knew that he had no sympathy whenever he was hungry, looking for his prey. The kitten mewed and was vigorously tugging at the rope. She would do everything possible to protest her being used as a bait for a wanted, notorious flesh-eating animal.

Gedu adjusted his gun and warned his son not to swat the biting tsetse-flies, no matter how painful their biting might be. He had been chasing the hyena for over five years. The hyena, agile and cunning, always escaped. In addition to that, he had killed more than a score domestic animals, including a bull which was meant to be sacrificed during the festival of Ancestors, otherwise known as "Egungun Festival." Then he and his friend, Kakadu, searched the bushes for weeks without a spoor of the notorious carnivore. It was the determination to kill this hyena that made Gedu erect a hunting but as a stepping stone to finding out the hyena's hideout.

Both animals looked at each other. As the hyena made a move, the poor kitten mewed, her eyes twinkled successively: apparently accusing the hyena why he should prey upon something whose freedom had been interfered with. The hyena, sensing the accusation, walked away with feline grace. He had decided not to attack the bait.

Gedu aimed at him but it was too late. The best time to have shot a dangerous beast could have been the time he was ready to attack his bait. At best, when he must have begun to eat his bait.

"Pa, why didn't you shoot him?" asked Raradi, as he wiped his face with the back of his hand.

"I could not shoot him because he was not in the position, ideal to be shot. But I swear; his days are numbered. I shall not eat or drink until my bullets are buried in the skull of that nuisance. I want to be the first hunter to kill that hyena," promised Gedu Ajanaka.

"Does it mean much to your life by killing that enormous animal?"

"Yes. Killing that notorious hyena, means I would become a title-holder in Oyako village, sitting among the Very Important Elders. Added to this is the fact that I would be regarded the most courageous hunter in the rainforest. Also, I would be carried shoulder-high around the village. I stand also a chance of becoming one of the decision-makers. Old and young would respect me. And I could marry as many wives as I please in this land."

In the afternoon, around 12.30, Gedu and his suave son sat by the foot of the araba tree. The rain had ceased. While father was smoking his pipe, the son was resting on a sheep leather-mat, munching a fried snail. To Gedu's right was his gun, put on his hunting bag, made of leopard skin.

He had promised never to drink or eat, and apparently he would keep his promise. Reneging on whatever is said is not common in old Yoruba land. He would wait till evening when the hyena would come out of his hideout, looking for his preys. He wondered why the carnivore had refused to make his laughing cry. Now he stood up and traced the footpath of the wild beast to a cave whose dark interior seemed to lead to a depth of about five yards. He stood there momentarily thinking of what to do next. There was nothing he could do now. The hyena would come out when he thought there was no danger of any sort around. That's something to do with the law of self-preservation.

He came back and sat under his temporary abode, his face wrinkled with anger. His son, seeing his countenance, knew that his father was not destined to succeed that day. He did not seek the mind of the Ifa diviner, nor did he ask Ogun to clear the way for him. How could he then succeed? He also knew that his father was not a trained hunter. He simply decided to become a people's hunter just because his own father had been a successful hunter before he died. That was the last hunter known to men and women, young and old in Oyako village. That was the only hunter who used to kill quarries with his poisoned spear. To be a successful hunter in Oyako village, one has to consult the oracle. That, Gedu had failed to do. He simply believed in luck and his unusual machismo. Also, he believed that *what one man can do, another man can do it.*

At around 3 pm, he took leave of his son and went step by step to the cave again, thinking that the wild animal would be seen coming out of his cave. He waited for almost thirty minutes without seeing the shadow or the movement of any creature.

On his way back, he saw a tribe of drills near a thicket. He was not interested in anyone of them. He was also not interested in a large fowl preening atop an Iroko tree. A few yards before he reached the araba tree, he saw a gazelle. Aiming, he fired and killed him instantaneously like a professional hunter. His countenance glowed, beaming with satisfaction.

Suddenly, appeared Kakadu. Irefully and loudly, he asked, "Why on earth did you leave Akoko alone in your hunting but without a repast in his possession? Why did you not tell him to follow you? Did you want him to be devoured by the hyena? Tell me: why did you leave him alone? I advised you as a friend to stop your inhuman scheme."

Gedu looked at his son. His son looked at him. He had no answer to any of Kakadu's questions. A twinge of conscience had begun to prick him. And when he fully realized what he had done, he blushed. He turned away his face to hide his blushes. It was dawned upon Kakadu that his friend had used Akoko as a bait for the hyena.

"I've nothing to hide, my friend. It is true that I had used Akoko as a bait for the hyena. However, I have vowed to kill the hyena and become one of the titleholders in Oyako village."

"It is a murderous act to use human beings as baits for an animal just because of a title. Is this the way your father achieved his popularity?"

"My father is different from me. I am different from my father. When my father was alive, he used his poisoned spear to kill animals. Gone were those days. Today, I used nothing but my powerful gun. Is my gun not ready to kill that notorious animal?" He tottered to his feet like a person in a drunken stupor. Was he feeling hungry? Was he pixilated? All these questions crossed Kakadu's mind, for someone in his right mind could not have behaved the way he had behaved. For Kakadu, he seemed not to have realized the gravity of the crime he had committed. However, he had disappointed him. And now he remembered why Oyako village was invariably referred to as a savage village: a village where about half of its population of one thousand, still lived like the early creation. Quite a number of them believed that since man is created naked, man must live naked and die naked.

"Gedu, remember that whosoever kills his fellow human, shall be killed also. Let this be graven on your memory. I pray that the Almighty God will forgive you." Having said this, Kakadu left his friend and started to walk westwards, backing the glory of the sunset.

Meanwhile, Akoko was weeping having overheard the conversation between Gedu and Kakadu. In no time at all, he left his master's hunting but for the village. On getting home, he tried to cure himself of the shocking revelation.

"Pa, Akoko is not expected to be a bait for that wild beast. He is nice to you much as he is nice to me."

"I thought it would but it doesn't work."

"God would never let it work. Don't you know that killing Akoko, your very domestic servant, is like killing me, your very son?"

"Stop the nonsense. Who wanted to kill him? I didn't want to kill him. I only wanted the hyena to attack him."

"You wanted the hyena to attack him and kill him so that you could kill the hyena. Is that not what my father is trying to say?"

"Yes, that's what I'm trying to say."

"If Akoko had met his death that way, you could have been regarded as a murderer and the law could have seen you that way."

"Shut your dirty mouth. You don't know anything about the law of the jungle in which the servant is always at the mercy of his master. And you must not forget that necessity knows no law."

"It is easy for you to tell me to shut up my mouth but remember that Akoko has served you dutifully and faithfully all these ten years he had been with us. He has never been a recalcitrant. He has fetched our firewood. He has fetched water for us, both in rainy and dry seasons. He has weeded our compound. He has worked on our farms. He has grown our macrobiotic food crops and harvested them. He has done everything which a young domestic can do. In spite of all these, you intended to repay his faithfulness with a diabolic act.

"Don't you know that Akoko still remembers that he became your domestic on the death of my grandfather? He knows that my grandfather could not have thought of using him as a bait. I think Akoko deserves a better treatment than this diabolic act, taken into consideration the fact that, unlike my grandfather, you are a well educated hunter. How I wished my grandfather lives to witness how his obedient servant had wanted to meet his death! Oh God, this is too ..."

Tears in eyes, Raradi stopped. His father was looking agape with amazement. He seemed to be asking: When did my son start to grow a flippant tongue? Where did he have such an amazing courage? Has he forgotten that in this village, no matter how savage the people might be, children must think twice before accusing their parents? He thought of what to do with his son. He would punish him, he promised. He would tell him that he was the father and the breadwinner.

Raradi, a weedy young man, was sad. He thought of going home. Even if he had to go home, there would be no one to comfort him, for he had no mother, no brother or sister. He was the only issue of his mother. His mother was found dead nine moons ago. That was the first time when he had learnt about the notorious hyena which his father had determined to kill in order to become a titleholder. Perhaps he had used my mother as a bait for the hyena, he said to himself.

"Wait here for me while I go to fetch Akoko from the hunting hut," said Gedu to his son.

On getting to the hunting hut, he found that Akoko had left without a word or signal for him. He had left in tears, although, he would in no way be used as a bait for the hyena, at least that very day.

On coming back, he did not see Raradi by the foot of araba tree. He was worried. He started to race between the araba tree and his hunting but like someone tormented by insanity. He did that for nine times without seeing either the footsteps of his son or the footsteps of his servant.

Just as he wanted to sit down in his temporary abode, he discovered that his bait, the kitten, had also disappeared. He was boiling over with indignation. He looked aimless and hopeless like a person stranded on an islet. Suddenly he heard a laughing cry, and looking behind a nearby thicket, he saw the giant hyena eating his kitten. In a moment, he cocked up his gun. In another moment, he released the lever and fired; zum, zum, zum; hitting the hyena in the chest.

The hyena, knowing that his life was in danger, picked up a race. Gedu ran after him, swearing by the name of his father that he would prefer to die in the bush than to go home without the notorious flesh-eating animal. While the wild animal was running for his dear life, making his laughing cry, Gedu was chanting some incantations with the aim of catching up with his prized quarry.

Having raced after the quarry for ten minutes, crossing hills, dales and a lake, he shouted, "help me catch him, help me catch him." Within seconds, there were animals and birds of every variety and of every description, which came out of their nests and hideouts with the intention of helping him. But on seeing that he was armed, ready to shoot one of them, they all beat a retreat.

Eventually the hyena came to a hilly blind alley whose sides had been barb-wired. Going forward was impossible. Retreating meant his death in the hands of his foe. He was thoughtless, his eyes burning like fire. He did not know what to do. But he had to do something, quickly too, if only he wanted to save his head from being smashed by the bullets of a man who had sworn by the name of his father to kill him in order to become a title holder.

Knowing that he would very soon have his back to the wall, like every creature who would take that moment to fight back, he yelped like a fox. Gedu stood still with fright, wondering why he had yelped instead of his laughing cry. There was no time to laugh now. Apparently, he had yelped to warn Gedu to go away or face the fight of the year.

Just as Gedu wanted to aim at him, the flesh-eating animal sprang on him with a thunderous peal that echoed for miles into the bushes. Animals and birds hearing that thunderous peal, came out of their hideouts to see what was happening. Some of them, on seeing that it was a tussle between a crazy hunter and a pitiless carnivore, disappeared. Those who did not disappear were those who were looking for their forage as the twilight was fast approaching. They included foxes, cheetahs, mice, hats, owls and vultures.

Down the hilly blind alley, Gedu and the hyena, rolled. Some trees and palms were bruised as they collided with them. Others were deracinated as they rolled down the hilly blind alley. Both of them were bleeding profusely.

While blood oozed from the chest of the wounded carnivore, Gedu's body was a horrendous and pitiable sight. The hyena had wounded him with his paws, so much that his earlobe was drooping. It was a gory sight in which blood was flowing along the blind alley like the flow of a river during a torrential rain.

The battle between human and animal continued, nevertheless. Both of them were exhausted, breathing heavily like a marathon runner. Sometimes they screamed; sometimes they squalled. Their cries rent the air. The peace of the bushes was disturbed. Everything was disturbed, as a matter of fact, beyond any shred of quandary, Gedu and the hyena seemed not to realize this. Each was fighting for his dear life. When Gedu could no longer withstand the hyena's onslaught, he resorted to defensive tactics, parrying his foe's paws. The hyena fought like a wild animal, he is. He bit Gedu's face and neck and they were all bleeding. His right eye had swollen and he could hardly see.

By now, it was around 8 pm, and the fireflies could be seen around with their phosphorescent light. The stellar light could hardly be noticed as the moon shone enchantingly. It was as though it perched on one of the iroko trees. Under such a wonderful moonlit night, two creatures, had vowed to fray endlessly.

Praa, praa, was the sound made as the hyena now decided to tear into pieces Gedu's hunting suit. In no time at all, he was stark naked. At this juncture, he thought of tearing himself away, and to look for banana leaves to protect his private parts. But the wild beast would not let him go.

The longer the fight lasted, the weaker Gedu became. This was a man who had eaten nothing except his breakfast of pap and akara. Only God even knew where he had got those energies to fight a wild animal like the hyena, up till now.

By the time they rolled to where the hunting but was, Gedu was looking more dead than alive. He looked very much like a bleeding lazar. Here, he thought for a second time, of Akoko. Had he been killed? Had he gone into hiding? Or had he gone to the village and reported him to Chief Abuja? Whatever happened to Akoko, he would take the consequences, if ever he survived.

By the time they rolled to the foot of the araba tree, Gedu had lost his gun as well as his hunting bag. He never could tell when and how he lost them. Again, he tried to tear himself away but his foe held him back. Getting hold of the rope to which his dead kitten had been tied, he whiplashed the hyena successively and the beast growled and squalled. He ran round the araba tree and Gedu ran after him like a person involved in a game of hide and seek. While trying to regain his strength, Gedu was bemoaning the loss of his son. Sad and dizzy, he wept, thinking that his son must have been killed like his kitten. Unexpectedly, the hyena leapt on him and the savage attack resumed again. Dispossessed of the rope, Gedu immediately resorted to his defensive tactics again. They rolled and rolled; twisting and curving like a snake. Gedu made sure that the wild animal had no access into his private parts. Between two mahogany trees, was a lake. They rolled into this lake, disturbing the peace of the fishes. Here, it was thought they would meet their death by drowning. But after a few minutes, they rolled out of the lake. The lake became reddish from the blood oozing from their wounded bodies.

A few hours after midnight, the King of Beast roared. What could that mean? A lion never roars in the midnight without a threat to his life. Seconds later, animals of every description were seen in an emergency meeting, headed by the King of Beasts.

"Hark, thou my subjects," said the Lion, "I have called you all these late hours of the night because of the continuous cries of two creatures that have been disturbing the peace of my kingdom since yesterday. I want you to tell me what course of action should be taken against these rebellious creatures, for I can no longer tolerate their lack of respect for this kingdom. Enough is enough." He looked around the gathering and then roared to silence the noise at the rear of the gathering.

"My opinion," said the fox representing all the diurnal creatures, "is to invite the two fighters and ask them why they are unruly and contumacious. We have to do something now since we all know that procrastination is the thief of time."

Said the elephant, in a trumpeting voice; "I will suggest that we endure til 6 pm today before we invite them. Maybe they will even settle their grievances before that time, who knows. However, we all know that everything that has a beginning has an end."

Standing up gingerly, the mouse said, "King of Beasts, I'm speaking on behalf of all the nocturnal friends of mine. I think action should be taken against anyone who breaks the law of your kingdom. I am saying this because many of you know that the best time for us to feed is during night time and we do not want our sleeping hours during the day time to be disturbed."

"I want everyone of you to look at me," said the bat. "As you know, I belong to the animal kingdom much as I belong to the kingdom of feathered creatures. The mouse had spoken the minds of all the nocturnal creatures in this kingdom but one thing I would like to say is that the king should make a law that anyone that disturbs the peace of this kingdom shall be made to work a whole year for all members of this kingdom. We have no law yet though, let's make one as early as possible. I thank you."

The lion roared again and the meeting was called to order. "All of you," said the king, "have spoken well, and sympathetically too. Inasmuch as there is no law yet, I will rule that we wait till 6 pm, as suggested by my deputy, the elephant. Is that alright with every one of you?"

The answer that came from most of his subjects was in the affirmative. The meeting came to a close about two hours before the first cock-a-doodle-doo.

The roaring of the lion and the rushing of the animals to the lion's palace, did not worry the fighters. They simply guessed that something was going on among the animals, but why and what, had no idea. Each of them had something to pay for not giving peace a chance. While Gedu had to pay dearly for his dream of becoming a titleholder in Oyako village, the hyena had to pay dearly for being the much sought after animal in the land. History would regard the two of them as prizefighters without a prize-ring.

It was the laughing cry of the hyena that woke the fire-birds and the nightingales from their sleep, as Gedu pushed the carnivore against a thorny tree. It was a daylight of a new day.

The aggression slowed down by afternoon because it was a sizzling hot day, and one could have thought that Gedu would give up the fight and search for his son and domestic servant, but he did not. The fight continued as before, though with less vigor. By now trees, plants and grasses had been forced to sleep as if a hundred elephants had been fighting to survive.

At around 2 pm, Akoko rushed to Kakadu's house and said, "I have come to say that I have not seen my master since yesterday."

"Didn't he come home yesterday?"

"No, he didn't."

"What about Raradi?"

"I have not seen him either."

"I think Gedu is a crazy hunter. How can one spend two days in the bush searching for a crazy carnivore? Akoko, let's go and look for him."

The two of them searched for him among the hills and valleys without seeing him or hearing the laughing cry of the hyena. Having searched for fifty minutes, they heard someone squalling, not far from the araba tree. They rushed and found Raradi under banana leaves. He had lost one of his legs! They carried him hoping that his father would be found nearby. There was no trace of him.

On their way home, not very far from his hunting hut, they found Gedu dead by the bank of the lake between the mahogany trees. Lying nearby was his gun and hunting bag. His body had suffered mutilation. Standing in the neighborhood were two vultures, apparently thanking the Creator for giving them something to devour.

Getting back to Oyako village, they went straight ahead to Kakadu's house. Raradi's amputated leg was replaced by an artificial leg. A few hours later, Gedu was buried under the shadow of a coconut tree in his compound, without the hunter's praise. He had been buried more or less like a villain. On the bark of the coconut tree were the following, scribbled by Raradi and Akoko, respectively.

Raradi: Although you've died a loser
you've fought like a brave hunter for a personal cause, without the thought of your only son.
May this dirge, a testimony
for the world of a poor child bereaved of his mother and father.
May your heart repent so that you could enter the Kingdom of God
And as you enter the Kingdom of God
do not forget to pray every day for your lonely one-legged child,
who would one day strive hard to bring a decent honor
To this compound/pleasance

Akoko: Sorry, sorry, sorry:
these words are heavy
in my heart of hearts,
for only yesterday did I
know your heart, a secret
death for me, plotted.
I write these for you to know
that I hold nothing against you
and even when I die today, I hope
you would smile as you used to do

while serving you conscientiously.
Good-bye, Master.

An hour before the fowls went to roost, Kakadu, Akoko and Raradi went to Chief Abuja's compound to tell him of what had happened to Gedu.

"Gedu is dead," announced Kakadu.

"Gedu, the would-be titleholder?" Asked Chief Abuja, surprised.

"Yes. Gedu, the hunter, the would-be titleholder."

"How did he meet his death?"

"It's a sad story," said Raradi. "My father wanted to kill the notorious hyena in order to become a titleholder. But his plan was diabolic. He had used his domestic servant as a bait for the hyena. But God saved his servant, Akoko. Shortly before the hyena attacked the kitten, his second bait, the hyena attacked me and broke my right leg. Look, now **I** have only one leg."

The Chief stood up from his faldstool and went up to him and saw that his right leg was artificial. He was astonished.

"If my father," continued Raradi, "had not been stubborn, he could not have been killed by the hyena. I did tell him before I lost my right leg that it was a crime against humanity to use a human-being as a bait for an animal just because he wanted to become a titleholder."

"I heard him and the hyena lunging it out with each other for almost twenty four hours. Pitiably enough, there was nothing I could do to help him. The loss of my leg made me powerless. In order not to be devoured by the notorious hyena, I had to spend hours under banana leaves until Kakadu and Akoko came at the time when I was about to pass on. The hyena was more powerful and because he was more powerful, he succeeded in killing a hunter who had used a human-being as a bait for his killer."

"Akoko," said Chief Abuja, "I wanted to ask you why you never made use of your sixth sense. I drop the question. Now I ask you: why did you not protest, on knowing that your life was in danger?"

"In this land, a domestic slave has no right to protest to his master even if he is to be thrown inside a fire."

"Firstly, I will say you're not a domestic slave but a domestic servant. Secondly, you're a human-being and every human being has a right to protest. I am the Chief of this village. My constitution has no place for slavery. Do you understand me?"

Moistening his lips, said Kakadu, "I am the one who met him in his master's hunting hut waiting to be devoured by the hyena. I saved his life by telling him to leave the hut. And I advised Gedu to put an end to his machination. He could not have died if he had listened to my humble but humane advice."

"If my father," said Raradi, his eyes filled with tears; "had listened to my words, he could not have died. I spoke to him angrily and I even looked into his eyes. Normally a son is not expected to look straight into the eyes of his father. But I did that in order to let him realize his mistake."

The Chief shook his head left and right. He was still surprised. Without wasting time, he called an emergency meeting of the title-holders and Elders. In his address, he said, "I have called this meeting in order to announce to you the death of Gedu, the hunter who had vowed to kill the notorious hyena in order to become a titleholder in this village.

"Under the happy medium to which you've known me for many years, I will like to say that as from today, no one shall come to me with the head of a lion, or the head of a tiger, or the head of a leopard, or the head of an elephant, or the head of a python, or the head of a swordfish, in order that one of the traditional titles of this land could be bestowed on him.

"I know it is an act of courage or bravado to kill an animal which no one has ever killed before. I know a hunter is worthy of a reward if he brings home a python. I also know that it is praiseworthy if a hunter succeeds in bringing to this village a lion and a lioness. But today, an end has to be put to that kind of worthiness.

"To have one of us meeting his untimely death just because he wanted to become a titleholder by hook or by crook is not a good omen for this village. To think that the deceased lost his father barely three years ago is heart-broken. To think that the sudden disappearance of the deceased's wife, is barely nine moons ago, is very sorrowful. To have the leg of his only son amputated, in perhaps a melancholy story for the progeny. To think of using a human being to bait the hyena, the only carnivore, yet to be killed in Oyako village, is certainly inhuman, satanic, devilish, barbaric, disgusting and preposterous.

"Many people outside this village believe that almost half of its population of one thousand are savage: that the village intends to get back to the pristine simplicity of the Early Man. But if one takes a critical look into the history of this village, one will find out that most of the machinations have been carried out by the so-called educated Oyako villagers who had spent years in schools and colleges. Tell me: what have we gained from them? Why should an educated hunter intend to use his domestic servant as a bait for a wild animal? Why should the so-called educated and civilized ones seen to be more dangerous than the so-called savages who prefer not to have any contact beyond their world of destiny?

"Yesterday, we were armed with clubs and spears; today we are armed with guns. Do we use our guns to kill the wild animals that threaten our lives, or do we use them to kill our opponents in order to obtain a title, to have power, or to be rich? These are some of the questions you have to answer on leaving this place.

"As said earlier, no title of this village shall be bestowed upon anyone just because he had succeeded in killing a wild beast. This is going to be announced to everyone, young and old in this village. Let's make a decent history for our village. Let's stop any kind of generation gap.

"As from this moment, the title of this land shall be bestowed on whosoever has the love and the energies to produce the much-needed staple food, such as yams, coco yams, sweet potatoes, gari, plantains, bananas, carrots, pawpaw, rice, millets, etc."

Chief Abuja rose and others rose too. A scenario that the coming generation which is going to make the world a better place for our progenies: had been prophesied.

Consequently, Raradi and Akoko became sworn friends. As a matter of fact, they lived like twin brothers. While Raradi became a teacher for the handicapped, Akoko chose to become a palm-wine tapster.

One day, three years after the death of Gedu, Raradi decided to go with Akoko to tap wine. They went past the hunting but and then came to a forest of palm trees. As Akoko wanted to start tapping, he heard the laughing cry of the hyena. Gun in hands, he began to search for the animal among the willow trees and lilac shrubs surrounding the lake where Gedu was found dead, thirty six moons ago. Surprisingly, he found the helpless hyena sitting on his hind legs. Aiming at him, he shot him twice in the head. The carnivore lay dead. Around his neck was a ring. Attached to the ring was the following note:

"I, the King of Beasts, order the hyena to report to you, having been found guilty by the Animal Kingdom for taking the lives of two creatures; and fatally wounded the third."

Without wasting time, the two friends managed to carry their quarry. Slowly but steadily, they trudged along the only service road between the hunting but and the Oyako village until they reached Chief Abuja's compound.

"Akoko, when did you become a professional hunter?" asked Chief Abuja, on seeing the gargantuan hyena.

"I have never been one but today, people will say I'm one," answered Akoko, with a winsome smile.

"He killed him with my father's gun," said the one-legged Raradi.

Looking like a corker, nay a cockalorum, Chief Abuja, "The enactment three years ago is that no title shall be conferred on anyone who comes to my compound with a head of an animal. You are exempted from the enactment because your case is not only different but also sympathetic."

A week later, Chief Abuja made Raradi butler of his compound. The title of a raconteur with a twist of a fairytale, under the headword of folklore was conferred upon Akoko. In order to excel in the art of storytelling, the Chief sent him to the surrounding villages and towns collecting anecdotes, folktales, legends and mythologies, specializing in dramatic ironies.

Chapter Fifteen

On Folk Animism

NOT LONG AGO WAS it proved scientifically that every culture is shrouded in, and animated by nothing but animism, the sole belief that all life is produced by a spiritual force or that all the natural phenomena have souls. In other words, every culture in the distant past was steeped in animism, as every culture was/ is steeped in folklore, the headword for fairytales. Those ancient cultures were contented with the world around them and the world around them was the only kaleidoscope through which they perceived their days and nights, physically and spiritually.

The general perspective or notion is that animists believe that natural objects such as the sun, the moon, the mountains, the rocks, the rivers, the trees and the earth have souls. And that those natural objects are worshipped by ancient people, professing ancient (not primitive) religions. In his anthropological research which is contained in his book, *Primitive Culture* (1871), Sir Edward B. Taylor asserted that animism is a belief in spiritual beings. He inferred by saying that inasmuch as animists believe in spiritual beings suggests that all human cultures have a belief in, and must have practiced animism; which brings us to the analysis of our first paragraph above.

As we have noted in the preceding chapters, the Yoruba people never practiced animistic religious beliefs since the dawn of history. To them, Creator-Philosopher Olodumare is the highest omnipotent, omnipresent and omniscient Being. In the hierarchy and other male and female mononymous divinities like Oduduwa, Obatala, O'Sango, O'Sopono, Osun, O'Yemoja, Ogun, Orunmila, O'Esu, Oya, Olokun and Oshosi are junior and answerable to him. However, this does not mean that the Yoruba do not believe in animism, per se. This signifies how down-to-earth the Yoruba religion was before it was swallowed up by a foreign composition of beliefs. Does Thomas become an animist by reading the messages in the Ifa-Ife's Book of Enlightenment, the Bible and the Quran? The monosyllabic answer is no. The fact that Thomas believes that those Holy Books are attributed to Creator-Philosopher God, does not make him an animist. But if he believes that the soul of Creator-Philosopher God dwells in those Holy Books, then, it is then he will be stigmatized as an animist, from the religious points of view.

The form of animism to which the Yoruba people adhere to since the creation of the holy city of Ile-Ife is folk animism in which all the natural objects in a folktale have souls. We must remember thousands of our fairytales in this connection. These natural objects (shall we say creatures) can move, talk, wink, dance, work, play, eat, drink and perform all human functions.

Fundamentally, and like Pythagoras and Plato philosophies, the Yoruba folklorist believes that there is an immaterial force that animates the universe. The folklorist believes in spiritual beings concerned with human affairs. Our research lets us know that fairytales were created or invented in the 13th century by Gervase Tilburn, a Briton. Later in 1846, folklore was coined by another Briton in the person of William Thom.

When Did Fairytales Start in Yoruba Land? There is no one who can say exactly when fairytales began in Yoruba land. They must have begun hundreds of years before they were invented or invented in the 13th century by Gervase Tilbury. Fairytales are as old as the firmament that opened its door to the first batch of fairies (fairies and fairy-beings) (masculine and feminine) upon the earth in numbers, numerous in numbers. In order to imagine how numerous they are, D. O. Fagunwa referred to them in thousands, in his novel *The Brave Hunter in the Forest of a Thousand Fairies* published in 1938.

Additionally, our keepers of traditions believe that there are, from time to time, fairies and fairy-beings guiding every household in Yoruba land. To all intents and purposes, the story of the folktales is the story of that never ends. It is the story that is tied with the creation of the world in general and the creation of the Yoruba people in particular. With stress and rhythm, the creation story is shrouded in magic but not like the magic powers of the fairies and fairy-beings, the midgets, the diminutive and the small entertainers and beguilers of our children in particular.

Because folk animism is so prevalent in Yoruba culture, there is no folktale told without some element of natural objects, acting or behaving like humans. While Abiku (the wanderer child who dies and returns again and again to torment its parents) is the most celebrated phenomenon with respect to folktales in the spirit world, the tortoise, the folk hero and the fabled protagonist of antiquity of Yoruba folktales is the most phenomenal folklorist in the fairyland of fairies. The fairies which occupy most of our children's literature are entertainers in their own right. The fairies, the delicate and small beings with supernatural or magic powers are Ijapa's favorite or the commonest characters in his many stories that beguile children. Often than not, children ask for more of such stories. Because some the fairytales do not only make children's eyes moist, they make their hair stand on end, as well. The following is one of such folktales which beg the question of folk animism.

"The tortoise rules the world," is the slogan in the town, called Bojiboji. The tortoise, the ruler had his kith and kin around the world. If the tortoise rules the world, why is it that he cannot rule the rain, people would murmur, wryly, ruefully.

First, the eastern part of the sky was half-covered by the rain-bearing clouds. The people of Bojiboji thought it would rain but it never rained.

Second, the rain-bearing clouds moved to the western corner of the sky. The people of Bojiboji thought it would rain but it never rained.

Third, the rain-bearing clouds drifted to the southern part of the sky. The Bojiboji people waited anxiously for the rain to come but the rain never came.

Fourth, the cumulus moved to the northern part of the sky. The thunder grumbled and growled. The earth trembled. The people held their hands together, hoping and praying. They believed, as before, that whenever the thunder took the trouble to grumble and growl, the rain would fall, sometimes so heavy that it could knock dead a fowl. But this time, the rain simply defied all expectations in spite of the thunder's warning.

If the rain did not fall in the next three months, the people of Bojiboji would have to leave the town for another settlement in search of water, for it had now been one year since the people had witnessed any droplets of water from the firmament.

Two weeks later, the people decided they would stay put, come what may. Some still believed the tortoise could rule the rain. Others were prepared to nail him down with a slap on the wrist. They were ready to face the harsh elements. The birds also decided to stay. All the animals except the lion and his family members, namely the lioness, the tiger, the leopard, the puma, the jaguar, the panther and the lynx, had run helter-skelter. Some left for the north. Some went to the south. While a few decided to take shelter in the east, quite a number prayed to have their fill in the west.

The lion and his family were the last to leave Bojiboji, a town tormented by drought. On putting their heads together, the wild cats decided to go to the Morning-light, a region enriched with nine oases, with the hope of finding enough water to quench their thirst.

There was nothing in the first oasis. The keeper, a young tortoise of about 30, told the cats that he himself had only two gourds of water left before he would face the same fate like theirs.

A day later, they got to the second oasis. The middle-aged tortoise said she was sorry that she could not spare a cupful of what she had left.

The third oasis had nothing to offer. The couple regretted that they had no power to force the rain-god to let loose the rain as a matter of exigency.

The fourth oasis was about to dry up when they got there. The female keeper sympathized with them, saying had they come a week earlier, she could have had water for each one of them.

They left with sorrows but their hope of surviving the drought was not totally dashed. The chickens were preparing to roost by the time they reached the fifth oasis on the fifth day. Before the lion could open his mouth to say his mission, the oasis keeper said, "I know why you are here but there is nothing I can do to help you until the rain falls."

The quadrupeds left. Tired, thirsty but not broken. On the sixth day, they crossed a bridge in order to reach the sixth oasis. They met a couple, the owners of the oasis, each lying on a hammock, under the shade of a baobab tree, having enjoyed some hours of calisthenics. Nearby was an oasis, fast drying. The eight wild cats rushed to the bank and started to drink. Sooner than expected, the owners woke up and shouted, "Friends, this is not a free land to the kingdom of Creator-Philosopher Olodumare. By not asking, you have pushed into the oasis the spirit of our hospitality. The lion roared his anger. But this time, his roar could hardly wake up a babe from its slumber.

Wagging their tails in apparent disappointment and exasperation, the quadrupeds left behind what did not belong to them. After hours of trudging, they reached the seventh oasis. Here they met a tortoise who said that the elephant, his visitor had drunk the last but one hole of water in the oasis.

Again, the seven cats followed their leader, the lion. Again, they crossed a bridge and got to an area surrounded by dunes. Policing the eighth oasis was the tortoise, assisted by his friend, zebra. The two hosts were very kind to them. But their kindness produced neither food nor a cup of water for the thirsty throats.

On the ninth day, through thick and thin, the wild cats after three attempts, climbed to the summit of the highest ziggurat in the Morning-light. From the top of the mount, they could see the locations of the nine oases. Surrounding the ninth fertile place was a caravan of camels. Lying to the west of the fertile land was a brown cottage. Belching out of the cottage was a spiral of smoke. From that vantage point, the lion and his family members could see clearly the oasis and its surroundings. They could tell it was a fertile land. What they could not tell was whether or not they would be allowed a gulp each.

But no sooner they descended the mount than they saw the door of the cottage thrown open. On the threshold was the tortoise receiving his unannounced visitors with open arms. Consequently, he gave them water to drink. They all drank to their fill. Because their stomachs were craving for food, the tortoise offered them a basket of cherries, saying he had nothing to eat but cherries. All except the lion declined to eat the cherries. Minutes after he had finished eating, the lion developed a cluster of brown mane on the crest of his neck. Rather than being rebuked by his family members for eating the cherries that gave him brown mane, they thanked him for leading them to a fountain of life where life struggles, and vows to defeat death given the adequate and the right weapons of mass destruction cum mass decoration.

While leaving the brown cottage, the tortoise predicted that the lion would one day become the King of Beasts due to the fact that he was a brave leader. That was one of the few occasions in which the tortoise was given a slap on the back. It was the first time he had not asked that his kindness be requited. Also, he declined to rule the roast, neither did he utter that all his geese were swans.

Reciting one of his best, the tortoise said:

Tell me which culture
does not know fire burns.
Tell me which tradition
does not know the birds sing.
Tell me which oral culture
does not know the sun smiles.
Tell me which culture
does not know all things are subject to change
Tell me which oral culture
does not relish the music of the spheres
Tell me which human does not know animism, divine ancestors,
All Saints' Days have imprints in all cultures.

Again, it must be emphasized that the Yoruba people do not worship an iron, for example. They worship the Creator-Philosopher Olodumare, the Oversoul that creates, controls and animates that iron. In this regard, folk animism can be seen as an antidote to an animistic religion if the two practices are to be compared to each other on Yoruba points of view or perspectives.

THE TORTOISE'S FOLKLORIC CHANT

An edifying chatterbox
Claimed without a hearing
My obeisance
Made by your patriarchate.
Paradoxical sleeper
Betwixt a snore and sleep
Purchaser of aces sourcing from the
Realm of acme
Pedigreed field of roses
My obeisance I pay.
Dispenser of reasons for victories
Mythicized common sense
The folk hero and the fabled protagonist
Of antiquity in Yoruba folktales
A recalcitrant protagonist
Whose deuteragonists left
No choice but pray and amen/ase
My obeisance I pay.
Unpredictable folklorist versed in grandiloquence

On Folk Animism

Fretting under the axe of guillotine
A nexus betwixt Ifalogy and Ifadom
A doppelganger betwixt
Folktales and folk memories
This is my obedience
Charmed before your carapace.
Escapades stunted betwixt
Fictions and nonfictions
The rise and fall of the tide
A cock without a crow
A trickster fabled in paronomasia
Dovetailing with cunnings and dissimulations
A sponger in the house of hospitality
A reifier and feigner in a famished land
A passé-partout to the crises unsolved
A denouement for mysteries
Legend of comedy of manners
My obeisance I make.
A lotus-eater in a lotus-land of feints
An ageless fire-eater
An indispensable friend or foe
Pray, never will I become your dill
Even in the Day of Immortality, Sunday
Your dwelling of cowries nay mythopoeia
Sat you did, upon your high-backed chair
Reflecting, regaling upon the highs and lows
Life marked by vicissitudes of every description
Wearing a jewel of crowns
My obeisance, pray, I pay.

Animism is inseparable from a folktale just as a folk music is inseparable from the tradition. What make an oral story a folktale are the variants of the story that can be narrated over time (historically) and over space (geographically). It is noteworthy much as it is essentially that to be regarded a folktale, a story must be told over and over again.

Chapter Sixteen

The Roar Behind The Throne

As all the roads lead to the holy city of Ile-Ife, so also all the thrones have symbols. Each throne is decked out with carved symbols, carved symbols in the images of the lion. As some Yoruba will agree that owls and chameleons are regarded sacred in the land, so also some will acquiesce that lions are the only animals with which the Yoruba Kings and Chiefs have identified themselves since time immemorial. Postpositively so, for even today, some Obas who are otherwise known as the kings believe that as the lion is the King of Beasts, so also they are the kings of their subjects, as well as the lion, a mark of bravery and authority, as imbued affectedly by the ethos of the day.

Between the fourteenth and the fifteenth centuries, our anecdotal evidence indicated how the symbols of the lions were exceptionally used by the Obas throughout the Yoruba-land. For example, a crown was not consummated without a face or the head of a lion etched on it. The front gate leading to the palace was not complete without a full size carving of a lion sitting on both posts of the gate. There was no other place in the palace that displayed the presence of the lion more than the throne. In different styles and motifs, here the carvings of the king of beasts would resplendently display bravery and the wealth of the ruler. On the walls, there would be carvings, plaques and paintings of the roaring cat, completing the panoramic artistry. The king's throne was often referred to as *ibujokoalafia* (haven of peace).

Sometimes the artist would carve the lion to the number of panoplies, wives, children and domestic servants owned by the monarch. It is a commonplace to see the king's walking stick carrying the emblem of a lion, usually the head. The king's bravery and power could also be found in the way his umbrella was made—of the yellow grass and the shaggy, yellowish mane of a lion. It was not uncommon also to see a royal whisk made of a lion's mane. However, the roar behind the throne was more significant than the roar under the sun.

It is anecdotally evident that art and nature had combined to make the Yoruba palace a haven of beauty and that haven of beauty was unequivocally due to the aesthetic works produced by the artists and whose works made happy the Ile-Ife kings. Ironically, and as indicated in chapter three, it was one of those would-be happy rulers who ordered the near-wholesale slaughter of the city's artists, simply because the ruler waited too long before he could be coroneted the Oni of Ile-Ife. Not only that the artists were killed, the carvings of the lions and what the lions stood for were also destroyed by the temperamental and ireful king. Thus came to an abrupt end the Ife School of Art. The art and mystery of that time is yet to be discovered by archeologists.

To this day, there are several versions of the story, as to the exact time the lions first became the national animals of the Yoruba land; consequently resulting into the lionizing of the rulers. "It was a long time," said Adegoke in 1987, making no bones about it. He narrated a story of Karimolu, a seasoned hunter who met a number of animals and birds in Savanna-land, the habitat of the wild cats in Yoruba land; asking them to appoint the king of beasts for themselves. The last bird he met was Mr. Owl. He urged him to be the king, adding that the communities in the Savanna-land needed a king who was strong, brave, agile and fierce-looking.

Mr. Owl chuckled and hooted the following; "I suggest you take up that honorable post. You're a popular hunter. As a matter of fact, when one talks of popularity, you have no match. My friend, you are qualified to be the king of all these communities."

Mr. Karimolu waited for a few minutes thinking of what to say next. Clearing his throat, he said, "Mr. Owl, you are not only a sacred bird but also a wise bird. You're the wisest of all creatures that fly both in the daytime and the night-time. Why can't you then be the king?"

"I am sorry, my friend: I am not made for that. Finding a king in these communities won't be easy because none of us wants to become a powerless king who will be disobeyed by his subject. Moreover, kingmakers are needed before a king can be coroneted. May I suggest you talk to Mr.

Lion? He is not only strong and fierce-looking, he has the guts to behave like thunder. You will agree with me that whenever the thunder growls and roars, everyone of us trembles like the leaves in a storm. But none of us can roar except Mr. Lion. He can intensify his roaring and by so doing, we shall get used to him. Then we shall ask him to face Mr. Thunder whenever he threatens us with his cracking and roaring."

Mr. Karimolu was apparently pleased having listened to the minds of his friends. His face was radiant like the face of the sun. He confessed that Mr. Owl's suggestion was the wisest.

After three days of deliberation, he invited his friends and Mr. Lion to a meeting under an araba tree. Addressing the meeting, he said that his friends and himself, acting as kingmakers, had agreed to crown Mr. Lion as the first and everlasting King of Beasts in the Savanna land.

Replying, Mr. Lion said that if roaring was what Mr. Thunder considered as his royal symbol in heaven, under the canopy of the clouds, he would therefore consider roaring as his royal symbol on earth, under the canopy of the leaves. He therefore assured Mr. Karimolu and his friends that he could roar and that all the creatures in the Animal Kingdom would soon bear him out. He left the meeting after Mr. Karimolu and his friends had assured him that they would go around the communities telling one and all that he had been crowned the king.

No sooner the roaring cat was pronounced the king of the beasts than Mr. Karimolu asked him to follow him. He obediently followed the seasoned hunter to the king's palace. The king, on seeing the crowned roaring cat dignified his reply by saying that if the lion could rule over the beasts in the Savanna-land, it was his turn to bear sway over the lion and his people. Since that day, the king had added a new tassel of authority to his crown of jewels and arts in the calm strength of wisdom.

The second version of the story was about a hunter who freed a lion and a lioness after the animals had lived with him for many rainy seasons. By the time of freeing them, his friend, also a hunter, bought the wild cats and presented them to the king of Ile-Ife who was fascinated and charmed by the way the lion walked and looked, authoritatively. Consequently, the king asked the carvers and sculptors to portray the images of both animals as the members of the palace.

Our research shows that it was one of the Oyo kings who introduced the wearing of grass skirts as worn during cultural festivals; identifying his kingdom with the lion and his mane. Truly enough, wearing those grass skirts is like a story handed down from one generation to the other. Shortly before the Yoruba land was occupied by the British during the middle of the nineteenth century, a few royal masks and paraphernalia still embodied the bravery and the power of the lionized Yoruba kings.

Today, not many Obas (kings) identify themselves with the lion as it was the case between the tenth and fourteenth centuries. Howbeit, the lion still remains a royal cult of bravery, authority and adoration in Africa and other parts of the world, worldly, where the wild cat never exists, let alone the roar behind the throne.

Chapter Seventeen

Between the Influx And The Exodus

Shortly before the amalgamation of the Southern and the Northern Protectorates in 1914, the Southern protectorate of the present Nigeria saw a succession of powerful kings, such as Oba Aderemi I, the Ooni of Ile-Ife, who ruled from about 1850–1920, the Oba Gbadebo I, the Alake of Abeokuta, who ruled from about 1880–1920 and King Ovonramwen of Benin who reigned between 1888 and 1897. Others are King William Dappa Pepple who ruled Bonny between 1837 and 1864, King Jaja of Opobo who ruled from about 1860–1887, Nana of the Itsekiri, who ruled from about 1884–1916 and Oba Eweka I who ruled Benin City for a number of years before Oba Ovonramwen was coroneted in 1888.

Of the Benin and Yoruba Kings, one may not be too quick to affirm that they are blood brothers, sharing the same royal caul of kith and kin. That is why they freely interact on royal matters affecting both sides. While many writers will put them on the same page consanguineously and genealogically, a few will be hesitant to do so, due to the fact that the Binis have developed their own linguistic identity, known as Edo. However, the artworks of both ethnic groups are inextricably linked.

Prominent amongst the powers between the influx and the exodus are Oba Eweka II of Benin City who ruled from 1914–1933 and Oba Akenzua II who ruled the City from 1933–1978. They are the last most popular kings before there was a clash of interests between the past and the present. The past belonged to pre-Independence, while the present belongs to post-Independence.

The power between a bird's eye view which helps to shed light on the last two most popular and most influential kings in Yoruba land between 1920 and 1980; is a power to remember now, even forever. From all accounts, and by all means, the following Obas best fit the period in question.

Sir Oladipo Samuel Ademola II (1872–1962), the Alake of Abeokuta, was a rich businessman and newspaper owner. While living in Lagos, he became well known among the Egbas. At the age of 21, he started taking part in the politics of Abeokuta, which at that time (1893) had its independence guaranteed for a while by Britain in a treaty, and was governed by an "Egba United Government."

In 1904, Prince Ademola accompanied the reigning king Gbadebo I, on his visit to Britain at the invitation of the Colonial Secretary. His stay in Britain had a great impact on his government, as well as his youthful exuberance on becoming the king.

Following the death of Oba Gbadebo I on May 28, 1920, Prince Oladipo Samuel Ademola was chosen to be the new Alake of Abeokuta. He was crowned on September 27, 1920, at a spectacular ceremony, attended by the British governor and a jubilant crowd of over 10, 000.

Although annexed to the rest of Nigeria in 1914, Abeokuta retained much of its traditional system of government, which was changed by the influx of Christianity and Western education on one hand, and the exodus of much traditional values, on the other hand. However, his period saw many educated men appointed to the traditional positions of the kingdom. Favoring Western education, he allowed his son, Adetokunboh (born 1906) to go to England to complete his education, while providing help for schools and children of Abeokuta. He was awarded CBE in 1935 owing to his vision, dedication, ruling passion and pragmatism.

On July 29, 1948, Oba Ademola II abdicated his kingdom for two years as a result of a protest against him by the market women, organized and led by Mrs. Olufunmilayo RansomeKuti. Because he was missed during those two years of banishment, he was quoted as saying, "What affects the eyes, affects the nose."

Like Oba Ademola II, Sir Adesoji Aderemi II (1889–1980), the Ooni of Ile-Ife was a wealthy man before he came to the throne. He was chosen the Ooni of Ile-Ife (the most spiritual and the most legendary city of Yoruba land) in 1930, and was crowned Ooni on September 25, 1930. A luminary as well as a visionary, he modernized many Ife customs and traditions, and was physically and financially responsible for bringing educational opportunities to the ancient city. Oduduwa College, founded in 1932, is one of the many educational establishments he spearheaded. He was credited with the introduction of public amenities, not least the telephone (1930), pipe-borne water (1946) and electricity in 1955.

His diligence, geniality, energy and affability made him the indispensable ruler on various consultative bodies of the colonial government in the 1940s.

In 1936, he was awarded the King's medal for African Chiefs, and was made CMG in 1943. He was elevated to the old Western House of Assembly in 1946 and the Legislative Council of Nigeria in 1947. He was a delegate to the African Conference in London in 1948, and led Nigeria's delegation to Queen Elizabeth ll's coronation in 1953. He was a delegate to many other Nigerian constitutional conferences, from 1953–1958.

The king became an active member of Egbe Omo Oduduwa,the cultural organization, otherwise known as the School of Thought, founded in 1948 by the newly educated Yoruba elite, spearheaded by Chief Obafemi Awolowo. In 1951, the Egbe Omo Oduduwa gave birth to Action Group which ultimately became the dominant political party in Yoruba land.

In 1951, he was invited to become a central government Minister without portfolio regardless of his position as a king, and held the post until 1955. In 1954, he was appointed president of the Western House of Chiefs, a position he held until 1960.

Oba Aderemi II was the first Nigerian to be appointed Governor of Western Nigeria. He was knighted KCMG in 1961. Through his influence, Ile-Ife was earmarked the site for the Western Nigeria's own University, founded in 1961, which in 1987, became Obafemi Awolowo University.

A socialite and a "good mixer," he visited the Moor Plantation Agricultural Settlement of Ibadan, with the Emir of Ilorin, at an early date, and also met Obas from Ekiti Division, thereby breaking the tradition of secluded lives of the Yoruba traditional rulers. He attended the first national conference of the Obas held in Oyo in 1937, and hosted the second conference in Ile-Ife in 1938.

In his report in 1938, G.H. Findlay, the Senior Resident of the Southern Province of Nigeria, said, "Ile-Ife with a population of 48, 000 is administered by Oni, assisted by a Council of Chiefs. The Oni's crown is the oldest among the Yoruba-speaking people. He is an educated and sensible man with progressive and sound ideas and a keen sense of humor. The Oni's administration is sound. His personal supervision over the Treasury and the Department of the Native Administration and his control of the expenditure of his native treasury is less restricted than other native authorities."

One of his favorite proverbs/bywords is, "Omodegbon, agba gbon la fi da Ile-Ife." This translates to: "Youths are wise; the Elders are wise, consequent upon which Ile-Ife was created." He was respected throughout Yoruba land and beyond. Shortly before his death on July 7, 1980, he celebrated his 50th anniversary of his accession to the Spiritual and the powerful throne of Oni of Ile-Ife. To this day, he is still regarded the longest-reigning Yoruba King in recent times.

The treasury of Yoruba oral and written literature is a magnum opus in its own right. It contains hundreds of fairytales, proverbs, histories, fables, legends, rhapsodies, myths, mythologies, apologues, shaggy-dog stories, epics, poems, epigrams, essays, articles, panegyrics, research projects, et cetera, et cetera. It is Ijapa's fund of ideas, common sense and love for literature that gave birth to the magnum opus. It is Ijapa who confidently sauntered from an imaginary bridge of oral culture to a non-imaginary bridge of written culture, announcing him as the burden of proof, or as a witness to the tales from the remote antiquity to the present. In order to ascertain himself as the burden of proof, he sang two uncommon proverbs that extol the importance, the use and the practice of Yoruba proverbs in Yoruba land.

He who commits an atrocious act
Gives the person it is committed strength

This translates into: Eni tio dani loro
Fi agbara ko ni
The hands of the youth cannot reach the high shelf
So too the hand of the Elder cannot enter the gourd

This translates into: Bi owo omode ko ti to pepe
Be nani ti agbalagba ko le wo akeregbe

Conclusion

WHOSOEVER BELONGS TO THE circle of sciences and humanities cannot but release a breath of fresh air and verbalize that diffusion of knowledge through books and lectures is very crucial, so important that it can be regarded as sine qua non. That being said, let us reflect upon the saying that the Europeans had transformed their oral culture many years ago. They had examined and reflected upon many areas of learning and romanticized so much that they are able to pull out what is today known as philosophy. Their traditional religion had been replaced by Christianity. Their oral literature had graduated into written literatures many years ago. All these epochs of developments are meticulously studied in order to have a cutting-edge research of a comparative merit.

With an opal clarity, *Courting Mentalism (Philosophy), Religion and Literature* has succeeded in helping us understand that any lore that widens people's horizons and presents food for thought is the beginning of philosophy. Bertrand Russell (1872–1970), put it differently when he said, "To understand an age, or a nation, we must understand its philosophy, and to understand its philosophy, we must ourselves be in some degree philosophers."

With a perceptible nod of approval, we can now acquiesce that morality is the taproot and the fruit of religion, while character (iwa) is the faith associated with morality. If the origin and exercise of morality could be traced to the crown, then, it is only then we can expound that as the metonymy is the language of the crown, so also the language of the divinity is the language of the kingdom.

With a candid and humanistic quid pro quo, we will all believe that literature covers all and every kind of writing—oral, written, fiction and nonfiction. Surely, a good work of literature adds fullness to the meaning of life. For an imaginary literature which is the fountainhead of pleasure (like music rather than information) reaffirms the present and reconstructs the future. Thus it is not my meaning alone to verbalize that all the researchers (independent or academic) believe in the metaphysical concept central to Yoruba/African philosophy, religion and literature.

Nor is it my meaning alone to say that a writer is an artist and there is no particular toponym (place-name) for artists nowadays; no excluded colony or pleasance for people who do something with skill and good taste like painters, sculptors, weavers, dancers, singers, masons, graphic designers, illustrators, composers, carvers, photographers, drawers, poets, writers. All of them can be grouped as artists who belong to the same place-name (toponym), colony or pleasance.

What could have happened if Ifa had been developed into a Holy Book on the same footing with the Bible or Qur'an? What effects do Christianity and Islam have on Ifa? To the first question, everyone will agree that Ifa must have become a monumental book of philosophy, religion and literature which every culture will like to dwell upon. With 256 books and numerous chapters, Ifa is more voluminous than the Bible and Qur'an, put together. Like the Bible, it covers all the ethical aspects of human existence. The same is true when comparing it with the Qur'an. To the second question, the Bible and Qur'an have marginalized Ifa making it as though it never existed before the duo were written.

Let's go to the past and reconstruct what had been neglected, now that the center is no longer holding. We have escaped from the center of reality for too long. What can a man do without believing in his culture? A foreign culture cannot shelter him like his native culture, even if he is acculturated. We cannot afford to lose the sensibility of our very making, for whosoever loses his or her umbilical cord, loses everything; everything he or she owns.

We must remember that if we leave Ifa, Ifa will leave us, and the result of its turning its back on us will be catastrophic. Let's rally round so that we could show to the posterity the foundation and the salvation of our past and present existence, just as other faiths have shown to their posterity what they possess. Let us go to the basics: basics that must be born out of substance rather than emotion. There is salvation in spirituality. Inasmuch as the "holy books" are equal in the sight of Creator-Philosopher Olodumare/God, there is no logic of leaving one for the other. As "A" can be saved by believing in Creator-Philosopher Olodumare through the words in the Bible or Qur'an, so also "A" can be saved by believing in Creator-Philosopher

Olorun through the words in Ifa. Ifa must cease to be a chapter in the religion-philosophy of the Bible and other apocryphal writings.

For all it is worth, the Old Testament in the Holy Writ, in all its perspectives, in all its pluses and minuses, is garbed in the image and likeness of Ifa-Ife. The new Ifa-Ife today will be likened to the New Testament, which while jealously protecting its past, stands firmly to the dictates of the contemporary, embracing the fund of common sense.

Whether the hypothesis that Christmas is derived from Ifamas is valid or not, let's continue to remember that Ifa was established for its people. Like Christianity and Islam, we may not go out into the world converting "the unbelievers" or "the heathen" but we can tell the world/humanity that they have a chance, a goodly chance for that matter, as we pray the humanity will be benefitting from Ifa-Ife's corpus of informing, enlightening, educating, entertaining, inspiring, and above all, inoculating the body with the corporeal and spiritual happiness vis-à-vis wellness. If we continue to support Professor Wande Abimbola and his associates, it is not unlikely that every scholar and intellectual will be able to read and understand a passage in Yoruba literary work by the year 2025.

African literatures, African-American literature, African-Australasian literature, African-European literature, African-Latin-American literature, African-West Indian literature may be placed fidgeting on a three-legged table without the philosophy, the autochthonous religion and the literature of Ifa-Ife whose divinatory power is second to none in Africa and in Diaspora.

The mercury in the barometer of the Yoruba culture may be drying out if Ifa (the Bible), displaced by other holy books is not reconstituted and made available to all the traditionalists and researchers in oral culture. We shall all be stigmatized obsequious apostates if actions (in the name of Olodumare) are delayed till the coming generation. What is worth doing: is worth doing well, not least projecting what Creator-Philosopher Olodumare and Jesus Christ stand for; similarizing the Seventh-Day Adventist, the Mormon, the Jehovah Witness and the Scientology.

The reason to read and enjoy this book from page to page is not far-fetched. The plain reason is that it will be regarded as the first research project that succeeds in combining three disciplines under one cover. Its introduction to the general public will generate an inexhaustible interest, while its adoption as academic textbook is highly recommended to all the departments of mentalism, religion and literature. The least said the better.

References

The Twelve Most Prominent Yoruba Artists and Divinity-Philosophers, Proto-History Divinity-Philosophers, united by ties of consanguinity. Their Nobiliary Particles Are Phrasal and Praiseworthy.

Divinity O'Esu: He was a designer who built low-ceilinged dwelling places such as shrines, tepees and bungalows. In addition, artist Esu was a great philosopher-idealist who subscribed to the aesthetics of contradictions. That being said and comprehended, it is quite vivid still that the Yoruba put almost every evil tendency or malevolent practice in man down to his agency. He belongs to the Divine Hall of the Ancestors/Pedigrees and the Distinguished Notables of the Yoruba Pantheon.

Moremi Ajasoro: *Idealist Queen Moremi was the royal personage who saved Yoruba people from molestation and destruction, in the hands of the forest dwellers, known as the Igbo warriors, by sacrificing his only begotten son, Oluorogbo to goddess Olumerin. Now, an ancestor of consequence, she is being inducted into the Divine Hall of the Ancestors/Pedigrees and the Distinguished Notables of the Yoruba Pantheon.*

Divinity Obatala: He was a carver who carved the human skeletons. Artist-Philosopher-idealist Obatala or Orisa-Nla was a popular philosopher during the period of creation. A personage whose theophoric name relates to Olodumare, he was versed in human anatomy. He was a connoisseur of palm wine, whose gourd of palm wine never dried as the gourd refilled itself on its own accord. His drunkenness, (far from being called dipsomania) during which time he lost his calm strength of wits and wisdom, sadly and regrettably impaired his claims to seniority over divinity-philosopher king Oduduwa. He belongs to the Divine Hall of the Ancestors/Pedigrees and the Distinguished Notables of the Yoruba Pantheon.

Divinity Oduduwa: He was a designer and builder of bungalows and tepees. Artist Oduduwa, a pacifist, liberalist, transcendentalist, idealist, was a great reasoner: a forward-thinking who planted the seeds of enlightenment and founded the holy city of Ile-Ife. Thus he is the father of Yoruba folk philosophy. He was a pragmatic personage whose theophoric name relates to Olodumare. He belonged to the Divine Hall of the Ancestors/ Pedigrees and the Distinguished Notables of the Yoruba Pantheon.

Divinity Ogun: Ogun was a sculptor of stones and woods. Artist-Philosopher-idealist Ogun was a respectable and the classical commander-in-chief of iron and steel. He believes in the theory that there are good things in fighting as there are opportunities in tragedies. A fleet-footed man, he always sets out at dawn. His theophoric name relates to Olodumare, the Creator-Philosopher. As the cultivator of iron and steel, he believes that an artist, the person who is creative has more of inner expression and imagination than an average person. He added that no artist should allow his creative mind to be crushed, for any society that crushes the artist's creative mind, intentionally or accidentally, must have crushed an irreparable genius who is destined to lead to a larger phenomenon, given a chance. The crusher, whether an individual or a society, will soon become utterly lifeless without hope and progress and without any purpose and without any pride and honor in its cultural heritage that embodies indigenous knowledge. He reminded every artist to know that the bronze and the terracotta artworks created during the proto-Yoruba naturalistic civilization are examples of idealism in the global art industry or cultural civilization. In addition, he lets the world know that the terracotta artists of the pre-Christian era were the founders of the Art Guilds, the Cultural School of Philosophy, which today can be likened to many of Europe's old institutions of learning which were originally established as religious bodies. These guilds may well be some of the oldest non-Abrahamic African centers of learning to remain as viable entities in the contemporary world. The following is his renowned universal apotheosis:

OGUN CLEAR THE WAY FOR ME

Ogun, clear the road for me
In my journey, day and night
On my way to fetch water
Clear the road for me.
On my way to fetch firewood
Clear the road for me

On my way to fish
Clear the way for me
On my way to farm
Clear the way for me
On my way to gather fruits or snails
Clear the road for me
On my way to hunt the wild
Clear the way for me
On my way to worship
Clear the road for me
On my way to my kith and kin
Clear the road for me
On my way to the market, buying or selling
Clear the road for me
Divinity-Philosopher Ogun,
Clear the road for me
During the hot harmattan Dry Season
Perspiring like a lidded pepper soup
Pot on the fire
Clear the road for me
During the Rainy Season
Drenched to the skin
Like a chick in a downpour
Clear the road for me
Machete sheathed in peace time
Unsheathed in danger time
Divinity-Philosopher Ogun,
Clear the road for me
Whenever the road is spiky
Whenever the road tends
To become my driver
Whenever the road is treacherous
And famished for food
Divinity-Philosopher Ogun,
Give me your dexterity in all the instruments
Pertaining to arts, iron and steel
And let me be safe in using all the instruments
Made by you, cultivated by you,
Created in your name and honor. Ase.

He is a brave personage of the world, worldly, and belongs to the Divine Hall of the Ancestors/Pedigrees and the Distinguished Notables of the Yoruba Pantheon.

Divinity Olokun:Olokun was a designer and builder of bungalows and shrines along the seashores and other hydrous places. He was often referred to as the cultivator of thalassotherapy, is an important philosopher-idealist who is in charge of the hydrous places worldwide. In other words, he epitomizes oceans, seas and waters on the surface of the earth. He has an unflinching faith in watery places (without the mud) as life sustainers. His theophoric name relates to Olodumare. He belongs to the Divine Hall of the Ancestors/Pedigrees and the Distinguished Notables of the Yoruba Pantheon.

Divinity Orunmila: He was a designer and builder of shrines and bungalows. He was also a carver of boards of divination. Additionally, he was a sage of creative and interpretative mind. From the House of probity, divinity-philosopher Orunmila, is a knowledgeable philosopher-idealist whose oral magnum opuses are second to none amongst his peers. His passion for morality and rectitude did help to inspire the scions of the land to divorce and distance themselves from vulgar manners. His Midas Touch has turned divination into a global phenomenon. He is the father of Yoruba idealism, and his theophoric name relates to Olodumare. He is also the cultivator of Ifa-Ife Divination, known as the Body of Knowledge or the Book of Enlightenment that embodies psychology, religion, philosophy, mathematics, literature, sociology, anthropology, cosmogony, cosmology and other fields of human interests or learning. He was well up in mentalism, that is he was equipped with a creative and interpretative mind. A man of singular courage and honesty, he is revered for being sententious/gnomic. In other words, he is the most sententious of all the Yoruba divinities. He is considered by many Yoruba keepers of traditions as one of the few ancient Enlightenment thinkers. Gifted with the kingdom of thought and the kingdom of reasoning, he is a natural healer, a ventriloquist, and member of the Divine Hall of the Ancestors/Pedigrees and the Distinguished Notables of the Yoruba Pantheon.

Divinity Oshosi: He was a maker of catapults. He is a fleet-footed philosopher-idealist, versed in hunting and the art of hunting. He was a sharp shooter who never missed his target, or failed to find his hunted or quarries. He is credited to have introduced hunting to Yoruba land. His theophoric name relates to Olodumare. He belongs to the Divine Hall of the Ancestors/Pedigrees and the Distinguished Notables of the Yoruba Pantheon.

Divinity Oshun: She was a knitter and raffia skirt weaver in addition to being an amazing singer and dancer. Pioneer and cultivator of what is today known as feminism, divinity Oshun is one of the youngest female philosopher-idealists. She characterizes character, probity, beauty, sweet waters and productivity. In short, she is a virtuous feme convert who never carries despair or meanness in her brave heart. She identifies herself with River Oshun, a river said to be a blessing to mothers and mothers-to-be. She is an empathic and kind-hearted feme convert of the world worldly, and she has an unflinching faith in rivers (without the mud) as life-sustainers. Her theophoric name relates to Olodumare. She is a member of the Divine Hall of the Ancestors/Pedigrees and the Distinguished Notables of the Yoruba Pantheon.

Divinity Oya: She was a raffia skirt weaver and maker of calabash bowls. She is foremost amongst the Yoruba female philosopher-idealists. She identifies herself with River Niger. In other words, River Niger is her alter ego personified by her. She has an unshakable faith in River Niger (without the mud) as a life-sustainer. Her theophoric name relates to Olodumare. She is a member of the Divine Hall of the Ancestors/Pedigrees and the Distinguished Notables of the Yoruba Pantheon.

Divinity O'Sango: Sango, the originator of the Festival of Lights, he was a designer and builder of bungalows. He was the philosopher-idealist who represents fire, lightning and thunder. In his lifetime, he was the third Alafin of the Oyo Empire. He belongs to the Divine Hall of the Ancestors/Pedigrees and the Distinguished Notables of the Yoruba Pantheon.

Divinity O'Soponna: He was a designer and builder of tepees. Philosopher-idealist Soponna typifies destruction upon malevolence. He acts and fights for whosoever needs his help and that person must possess a contrite heart. He is a member of the Divine Hall of the Ancestors/Pedigrees and the Distinguished Notables of the Yoruba Pantheon.

Divinity O'Yemoja: She was a raffia skirt weaver and calabash-bow maker. She is a respectable female philosopher-idealist who represents the ocean, the essence of motherhood and a protector of children worldwide. She has a passionate faith in watery places (without the mud) as life-sustainers. She was a passionate peacemaker among mothers. She belongs to the Divine Hall of the Acestors/Pedigrees and the Distinguished Notables of the Yoruba pantheon.

The proto-history philosopher-idealists and artists have all impacted the meaning of the Yoruba people, their kingdom of thought, as well as their kingdom of reasoning.

Post-Oral Divinity-Philosophers

Chief Moshood Abiola (1937–1998): The fourteenth Aare Ona Kakanfo of Yoruba land (generalissimo), installed on He was a philanthropist, liberalist and a political philosopher.

Chief Gani Adams (1970-) The current (fifteenth) Aare Ona Kakanfo (generalissimo) of Yoruba land, installed on October 14, 2017 by Oba Adeyemi III, the Alafin of Oyo.

Sir King Adesoji Aderemi (1889–1980): He was a discreet, respectable and peace-loving traditional king of the holy city of Ile-Ife and political philosopher. He was a social democrat, pacifist and liberalist. He vouchsafed for the fundamental unity that put an end to the schisms that hitherto existed among the royal houses in Nigeria.

Oba Efuntola Adefunmi (1928–2005) Oba Adefunmi was an idealist and a lover of Yoruba/African royal values. He was the first African-American to be coroneted a king by a Yoruba royal authority outside of Yoruba land. In order to bring closest to the hearts of African-Americans in Diaspora, he founded the Oyotunji African Kingdom (as a New World Yoruba initiative) in 1970.

Adegoke Adelabu (1915–1958): A writer, a journalist and the first chairman of Ibadan District Council. He was a charismatic pacifist.

Chief Samuel Ladoke Akintola(1910–1966): A national and international orator, and a gifted user of Yoruba proverbs and aphorisms. He was both a liberalist and pacifist.

Chief Obafemi Awolowo (1909–1987): A dynamic political philosopher who made Western Nigerian civil service one of the best in the world. He was considered a social democrat, a revolutionary, pacifist and liberalist. He is a scenarist, often referred to as the President Nigeria never had.

Beier, Ulli (1922–2011): He was a well-travelled scholar, researcher, writer and artist. UlliBeier was a connoisseur of the Yoruba literature, religion, philosophy and artefacts. Together with dramatist Duro Ladipo, he founded Mbari-Mbayo Centre in Ibadan-Oshogho in 1962. And in 1982, he founded and directed the Iwalewa House, an art centre at the Bayreuth University, Germany.

Chief Tai Bola (1898–1989): A local historian, liberalist, pragmatic idealist, pacifist, philosopher and keeper of traditions

Bishop (Dr.) Samuel Ajayi Crowther (1807–1891), he was the first nineteenth-century language and folk philosopher. The first Anglican African Bishop of the Niger Territory, he translated the English Bible into Yoruba language. He was, according to our record, the first religion philosopher of the land. Additionally, he was a pacifist, an abolitionist, a missionary who was on the vanguard of, and belonged to the Way of Enlightenment that emerged after the Yoruba wars in the 19th century.

D.O. Fagunwa (1903–1963): A writer and narrative, folk philosopher. He was the first Yoruba folk philosopher, employing metaphysics or naturalism to tell his stories.

Dr. Samuel Johnson (1846–1901): An influential classical Enlightenment thinker, he was a pacifist, liberalist, philosopher and historian. He was the first person to complete the historical writing of Yoruba land—A History of the Yoruba(s), published in 1921. He belonged to the Way of Enlightenment that emerged after the Yoruba wars.

Duro Ladipo (1931–1978) A popular international playwright and the author of Oba koso—the king did not hang. Oba ko so is a melodramatic play of how the famous king Sango was presumed dead but alive and kicking, as he became king of Thunder and Lightning. He was often referred to as a playwright whose mouth emitted fire while acting.

Herbert Macaulay (1864–1946): Doyen of Lagos politics, he was an astute political philosopher and pacifist. He essayed to turn the fears and scars of the Yoruba wars into intrepidity, the irascibility into rationality and the defeated into valiant survivors. These pacific efforts of his enabled him to found in 1944, a viable political party in Nigeria—National Council of Nigeria and Cameroons (NCNC), together with Dr. Nnamdi Azikwe. Also, he was the founding visionary of the Nigerian National Democratic Party (NNDP) in 1923, the first political party in the united Nigeria. He belonged to the Way of Enlightenment that was rapidly taking root after the Yoruba wars.

Hubert Ogunde (1916–1990) A pacifist, liberalist and prolific artist, he was an actor, playwright, theatre manager and musician who founded Ogunde Concert Party in 1945, the first professional theatrical company in Nigeria. He was the doyen of modern Yoruba /Nigerian playwright and dramatist.

Kola Ogunmola (1925–1973) He was the founder of Ogunmola Travelling Theatre in 1947. A gifted dramatist, actor, mime, director and playwright, he staged the musical version of Amos Tutuola's The Palm wine Drinker which was performed at the first Pan-African Culture Congress in Algiers in 1969.

Ajibike Ogunyemi: He is one of the many men who worked with Susanne Wenger to make Oshun Grove the artistic statement it is today. A prolific sculptural artist, Ogunyemi's work is known throughout Oshun state.

Twin Seven-Seven (1944–2011) Member of the Oshogbo School of Art Movement, Twin Seven-Seven began his art career in the 1960s in the workshops conducted by Ulli Beier and Georgina Beier in Oshogbo. A versatile and gifted artist, he was designated UNESCO Artist for Peace in 2005, in recognition of his contributions to the promotion of dialogue and understanding amongst peoples, particularly in Africa and in Diaspora.

Wole Soyinka: A liberalist and political philosopher. In embracing pacifism, he took delight in political activism, displaying an exceptionally discreet/tactful bravery. Soyinka is a multi-talented avant-garde litterateur. He was the winner of the Nobel Prize for literature in 1986, the first wordsmith of African descent to be so honored.

Chief Susanne Wenger (1915–2009) An exceptional artist, pacifist, liberalist and philosopher (a connoisseur of Yoruba cultural values and cardinal virtues), Susanne Wenger is instrumental to the formation of the New Sacred Art Movement otherwise known as the Oshogbo School of Art Movement. Due to her devotion, her wisdom and love for sculptural art and culture of the Yoruba land, the Osun Oshogbo Sacred Grove was declared a UNESCO World Heritage Site in 2005.

Post oral philosopher-idealists are the new age philosopher-idealists who have impacted the meaning of the Yoruba people and their metaphysics—philosophy of the mind. Educated in the modern age, they were able to promote the past so that the present can live to be wiser and the future wisest.

Philosopher-Idealist Kings

THIS IS A NUMBER of Yoruba philosopher-idealist kings who are always forward-thinking and bent on the kingdom of reasoning and kingdom of thought.

His Majesty Oba Adeyeye Enitan Ogunwusi; the Ooni of the holy city of Ile-Ife: assumed office on October 26, 2015. A pragmatic idealist, he is in the vanguard of idealism cum realism, as enshrined in his protocol of world tours

His Majesty Alafin of Oyo, Oba Lamidi Adeyemi III: assumed office in 1970.

His Majesty Alake of Egbaland, Oba Adetoun Aremu Gbadebo: assumed office in 2005

His Majesty Awujale of Ijebuland, Oba Sikiru Kayode Adetona: assumed office in 1960

His Majesty Oba of Lagos, Oba Riwalni Babatunde AremuAkiolu: assumed office in 2003

His Majesty, Olubadan of Ibadan, Oba Saliu Adetunji: assumed office in 2016

His Majesty, Ataoja of Oshogbo, Oba Jimoh OlanipekunLarooye II: assumed office in 2010

His Majesty, Ewi of Ado-Ekiti, Oba Rufus Adeyemo Adejugbe Adesanmi III: assumed office in 1990

His Majesty, Deji of Akure, Oba Aladetoyinbo OgunladeOdundun II: assumed office in 2015

His Majesty, Osemawe of Ondo, Oba (Dr.) Victor Adesimbo AdemefunKiladejo: assumed in office 2006.

His Majesty, Owa Obokun of Ijesha, Oba (Dr.) Gabriel Adewale Aromobani II: assumed office in 1982

His Majesty, Soun of Ogbomoso, Oba Oyewunmi Ajagungbade III: assumed office in 1973

His Majesty, Olowo of Owo, Oba Folagbade OlateruOlagbegi III: assumed office in 1999

His Majesty, Olugbo of Igbo-Kingdom, Oba Frederick Obateru Akinrunta: assumed office in 2009

His Majesty, Oluwo of Iwo, Oba Abdurasheed Adewale Akanbi Telu I: assumed office in 2015

Yoruba Calendric Days and Months of the Year

DAYS OF THE WEEK

Sunday	Aiku
Monday	Aje
Tuesday	Isegun
Wednesday	Ojorun
Thursday	Ojobo
Friday	Eti
Saturday	Abameta

MONTHS OF THE YEAR

January	Sere
February	Erele
March	Erena
April	Igbe
May	Ebibi
June	Odudu
July	Agemo

August -- Ogun

Setembe -- Owewe

October -- Owawa

November-- Belu

December--Ope

GLOSSARY/LEGEND

Adire	Popular Yoruba cloth
Agbada	Voluminous Yoruba robe
Ase	The positive power or energy that makes things happen
Aso-oke	Valuable Yoruba attire
Ayo	Yoruba philosophical game, played by two
Holy-Gourd	A symbol of necessity conferring material, spiritual and mystic benefits. (Author's invention.)
Mo wa	I have come: baby's first cry/sound of life
Sasarawa	An idyllic dwelling characterized by tranquility, bliss, beauty and longevity. (Author's invention.)

Author Bio

FORMER RESEARCH FELLOW, HARVARD University, former Director, Institute of Creative Writing, author of The Aesthetic and Moral Art of Wole Soyinka, Yoruba Idealism, and a good few; recipient of a Poetry Golden Trophy, recipient of the 2021 Nonfiction Fellowship Award from the Writers' Room of Boston, recipient of the 2023 Humanities Grant from the Massachusetts Cultural Council, Yemi D. Ogunyemi (also known as Yemi D. Prince) is a beaut aphorist and a luminous literary philosopher whose work reflects the savvies and radiance of his spirit, and always fascinated by letters, books and the power of words. His corpora which is a blend of Yoruba folk philosophy, autochthonous religion and literature, is purposed to inform, enlighten, educate, entertain, inspire and above all, inoculate the body with the ingredients of wellness and happiness. While he believes that good literature adds fullness to the meaning of life, he also believes that art, the marvel of ingenuity, a symbol of reality, is an expression of happiness, an application of human creative skill. His canon of over 70 titles includes fiction, nonfiction, plays, poetry and children's stories, likening the chiaroscuro found in them to the canons of good taste. His most recent work is Yoruba Idealism. His eBooks include The World, in a Fume of Pandemic Anxiety, Quid Pro Quo and Other Narratives and How to Erase Racism from the Minds of Humanity. Currently, he is working on The Study of Yoruba Classic Fairytales/Folklore and Literary Criticism.

Select Bibliography

Abimbola, Kola (2006). *Yoruba Culture: A Philosophical Account*, Iroko Academic Publishers, Birmingham, UK.

Abiodun, Rowland (2014). *Yoruba Art and Language: Seeking the African in African Art*, Cambridge University Press, Cambridge, UK.

Adegboyega, LatosaMabinori (2020). *The Holy Book of IfaAdimula, the Sacred Voice of God*, Safari Books, Ibadan, Yoruba land.

Appiah, Kwame Anthony (2010). *The Honor Code*, Norton, New York, London.

Asante, Molefi Kete (1987). *The Afrocentric Idea*, Temple University Press, Philadelphia,.

Awolowo, Obafemi (1981). *Voice of Reason*, Fagbamigbe Publishers, Akure, Nigeria.

Beiser, Frederick C (1987). *The Fate of Reason*, Harvard University Press, Cambridge, MA.

Berlin, Isaiah (2000). *The Power of Ideas*, Princeton University Press, NJ.

Bulfinch, Thomas (MCMLXXIX). AVENEL BOOKS, New York.

Butterworth, John; Thwaites, Geoff (2005) Cambridge University Press, Cambridge, MA.

Cahn, Steven (Ed) (2011) Thinking About Logic, Westview Press, Boulder, Colorado.

Deleuze, Gilles; Guattari, Felix (1994) What Is Philosophy? Columbia University Press, New York.

Dickens, Charles (2004) Hard Times, Pearson Educations, London.

Ducasse, Curt J. (1966) The Philosophy of the Art (2nd ed.) Dover, New York.

Eze, E. Chukwudi (Ed.), (1997), *Post-Colonial African Philosophy*, Blackwell, Oxford.

Eze, E. Chuckwudi (Ed), (1998), *African Philosophy (An Anthology)*, Blackwell, Oxford.

Fagunwa, D.O (1950), *Ogboju-Ode Ninu Igbo Irunmale*, Thomas Nelson and Sons, London.

Feibleman, James K (1973), *Understanding Philosophy*, Horizon Press, New York.

Giovanni, Nikki (1971). Scholastic, New York.

Gyegye, Kwame (1987). *African Philosophical Thought (revised edition)*, Temple University Press, Philadelphia.

Hacking, Ian (2002). *Historical Ontology*, Harvard University Press, Cambridge, MA.

Halbertal, Moshe (2012). *On Sacrifice*, Princeton University Press, NJ.

Hauser, Arnold (1959). *The Philosophy of Art History*, Knopf, New York.

Hountondji, Paulin (1983). *African Philosophy, Myth and Reality*, Indiana University Press, IN.

Idowu, E.Bolaji (1962). *Longman Nigeria Limited*, PMB 21036, Ikeja, Lagos.

Ingarden, Roman (1973). *The Cognition of the Literary Work of Art*, Northwestern University Press, Evanston, IL.

———. (1973). *The Literary Work of Art*, Northwestern University Press, Evanston, IL.

Karenga, Maulana (2004). *Kawaida Theory: An African Communitarian Philosophy*, University of Sankore Press, Los Angeles.

Laye, Camara (1966). *A Dream of Africa*, Dramouss Libraire Plon, Paris.

Makinde, Moses Akin (2002). *Awolowo as a Philosopher*, Obafemi Awolowo University Press, Ile-Ife, Nigeria.

———. (1984). *African Philosophy, Culture and traditional Medicine*, Center for International Studies, Ohio University, Athens, OH.

Melvin, Rader and Bertram, Jessup (1976). *Art and Human Values*, Prentice-Hall, Englewood Cliffs, NJ.

Ngugi waThiong'o (1964). *Weep Not Child*, Heinemann Educational Books, Portsmouth, NH.

Nkrumah, Kwame (1964). *Consciencism*, Panaf Books, London.

Nyerere, Julius (1974). *Man and Development*, Oxford University Press, United Kingdom.

Obama, Barack (2006). *The Audacity of Hope*, Crown, New York.

Ogunyemi, Yemi D. (2022). *Yoruba Idealism*, Peter Lang, New York.

———. (2018). *Philosophy and the Seeds of Enlightenment*, Vernon Press, Wilmington, DE.

———. (2017). *The Aesthetic and Moral Art of Wole Soyinka*, Academica Press,
Palo Alto, CA.

———. (2016) *The Birth of a Child in a Fishing Boat*, Langaa Research and Publishing Common Initiative Group, Mankon, Bamenda, Cameroon.

———. (2016). *Ajayi Crowther's Piano*, Diaspora Press of America, Boston.

———. (2010). *The Oral traditions in Ile-Ife*, Academica Press, Palo Alto, CA

———. (2009). *The Literary/Political Philosophy of Wole Soyinka*, Frederick, MD.

———. (2003). *The Aura of Yoruba Philosophy, Religion and Literature*, Diaspora Press of America, Boston.

———. (1998) *Introduction to Yoruba Philosophy, Religion and literature*, Athelia Henrietta Press, New York.

———. (1998) *The Covenant of the Earth*, Athelia Henrietta Press, New York.

———. (1991) *Studying Creative Writing in Nigeria*, Merlin Books, United Kingdom.

———. (2004). *Literatures of the African Diaspora*, Gival Press, Arlington, VA.

——— (2014). *The Literary Philosophy for the Year 2000*, America Star Books, Frederick/Baltimore, MD.

-——— (2003). *The Melodrama of the Last Word*, Publish America, Frederick/Baltimore, MD.

——— (2008). *My Gazar With My Geisha*, Outskirts Press, Denver, CO.

——— (2006). *The Anthologies of the Diaspora*, Publish America, Frederick/Baltimore, MD.

——— (2010). *Stealing Amongst the Citizens*, Publish America, Frederick/Baltimore, MD,

——— (2012). *M-A-S-T-A-M-A-N-D-A*, Publish America, Frederick/Baltimore, MD.

——— (2014). *Obama, the Pragmatic President*, Diaspora Press of America, Boston.

——— (2015). *Codes of Morality*, Diaspora Press of America, Boston.

Oluponna, Jacob (2011). *City of 201 Gods: Ile-Ife in Time, Space and the Imagination*, University of California Press, Los Angeles.

Pinker, Steven (2002). *The Blank Slate*, Penguin, New York.

———(2009). *How the Mind Works*, Norton, New York and London.

Osborne, Harold (1955). *Aesthetics and Criticism*, Routledge, London.

Sartre, Jean-Paul (1965). *Situations*, George Braziller, New York.

Soyinka, Wole (1976). *Myth, Literature and the African World*, Cambridge University Press, New York.

———(1988). *Mandela's Earth and Other Poems*, Andre Deutsch Limited, London.

———(2012). *Of Africa*, Yale University Press, New Haven, CT.

———(1981). *Ake, the Years of Innocence*, Rex Collings, London.

———(2006). *We Must Set Forth at Dawn*, Random House, New York.

———(1967). *IDANRE and Other Poems*, Methuen & Co., London.

———(1972). *The Man Died*, Rex Collings, London.

———(1965). The Interpreters, Heinemann Publishers; Portsmouth, NH.

Sparshott, F.E., (1963). *The Structure of Aesthetics*, University of Toronto Press, Toronto.

Stolnizt Jerome (1960). *Aesthetics and the Philosophy of Art Criticism*, Houghton Mifflin, Boston.

Tomas, Vincent (ed) (1964). *Creativity in the Art*, Prentice-Hall, Englewood Cliffs, NJ.

Thorton, John (1992, 1998). *Africa and Africans in the Making of the Atlantic World, 1400-1800*, Cambridge University Press, New York.

Walsh, Dorothy (1969). *Literature and Knowledge*, Wesleyan University Press, Middletown, CT.

Wiredu, Kwasi (1983). *Philosophy and African Culture*, Cambridge University Press, New York.

www.ingramcontent.com/pod-product-compliance
Lightning Source LLC
LaVergne TN
LVHW050644100826
845148LV00011B/1974